STATE AND STATECRAFT IN OLD JAVA

A Study of the Later Mataram Period, 16th to 19th Century

SOEMARSAID MOERTONO

STATE AND STATECRAFT IN OLD JAVA

A Study of the Later Mataram Period, 16th to 19th Century

EQUINOX
PUBLISHING
JAKARTA KUALA LUMPUR

Equinox Publishing (Asia) Pte Ltd
No 3. Shenton Way
#10-05 Shenton House
Singapore 068805

www.EquinoxPublishing.com

State and Statecraft in Old Java
A Study of the Later Mataram Period, 16th to 19th Century
by Soemarsaid Moertono

ISBN 978-602-8397-43-8

First Equinox Edition 2009

TABLE OF CONTENTS

APPENDICES

MAPS

FOREWORD

Mr. Soemarsaid Moertono was born in East Java in 1922 and entered the Indonesian Civil Service in 1944. In 1962, before he came to the United States, he was teaching at Malang in the Academy of Public Administration under the auspices of the Ministry of Internal Affairs. In 1964 he successfully submitted this study as a M.A. thesis in the Department of History, Cornell University.

For some years students at Cornell have benefited from Mr. Moertono's work, and the Southeast Asia Program has decided that a wider public should have the same advantage. We are grateful to the author for giving his permission for the publication of his thesis as a CMIP monograph. We are especially grateful to Mrs. Arlene Lev, who undertook the responsibility of editing the manuscript. She did so, in her own words, as "a labor of love," for Mr. Moertono, during his two years at Cornell, never failed to put his knowledge at the disposal of the many who consulted him, always displaying a modesty and charm which no one who knew him will quickly forget.

Several Indonesian Dutch scholars, as well as contemporary Dutch observers, have examined aspects of Javanese government during the Later Mataram period, but few studies are at present available in the English language. The outstanding exception, to which Mr. Moertono pays tribute, is the late Professor Schrieke's *Indonesian Sociological Studies*, Volume II, The Hague, 1957, which is a translation of some of Professor Schrieke's unpublished manuscripts. In addition to published Dutch sources, Mr. Moertono has used his own substantial knowledge of Javanese literature, and, as a result, the reader of this study has the sensation that he is being helped to see the situation in Later Mataram from within. The reader will become aware of the rich contents of the

Javanese sources, for which Dr. Th. G. Th. Pigeaud has recently provided a valuable survey in the first volume of his *Literature of Java*, The Hague, 1967. Perhaps students will be attracted to the study of the almost entirely unexplored Javanese context of Dutch activities in Java. Students of contemporary and near-contemporary Java will certainly wish to take into account the background of political ideas which Mr. Moertono has reconstructed and analyzed.

Javanese cultural resources, as this study makes clear, have been concentrated on what may be called the science of government, with some of its values defined in Indian literature but with its practice adapted to the scale and exigencies of life in Java. The prestige of the science of government was maintained in spite of Dutch rule, and it is appropriate that Mr. Moertono, a teacher of public administration, should have addressed himself to the subject.

Readers will use this study for a variety of purposes in addition to its contribution to the history of the Later Mataram period. For example, some of the technical terms for describing the attributes of kingship are derived from Sanskrit, and they are also found in Cambodian epigraphy and can be studied in Professor George Coedès' *Inscriptions du Cambodge* . Thus an aid is offered for the comparative study of government in earlier South East Asia. Another aspect of Mr. Moertono's work which may attract attention is his observations on the education necessary for the cultivation of suitable moral and practical qualities in the service of the king.

The reader may ask himself whether he is dealing with increasingly obsolete features of Javanese culture or with a culture which possessed the capacity for self-renewal. This is a question which cannot be broached until scholarship has advanced sufficiently to permit historical insights to be used more appropriately in the study of recent Javanese history. In the meantime, Mr. Moertono has shown that the *piwulang genre* of literature exemplifies a critical spirit. That the tradition was sensitive to contemporary needs is also suggested by the work of Raden Ngabei Ranggawarsita (1802-1873), regarded by the Javanese as the last great *pudjangga*. Mr. Moertono notes the suggestion that this person was influenced by Dutch scholars and administrators, and this circumstance may be interpreted as a scholar's facility for adjusting himself to new needs without deserting established values.

The continuing process of Javanese adjustment to so-called modern conditions lies outside the scope of this study. The author's achievement has been to illuminate the way Javanese political ideas, though assailed by an unfavorable environment, did not cease to command conviction. Above all, the sense of the dignity of public service and the attribution of high qualities to public servants survived. One may permit oneself the hope that Mr. Moertono will, in spite of his present heavy responsibilities, find time to continue his research into more recent times, once again helping his reader to see the subject from a privileged position inside the tradition.

O. W. Wolters

London, England
1 May 1968

ABBREVIATIONS

Bijdragen: Bijdragen tot de Taal-, Land- en Volkenkunde (van Nederlandsch Indië)

VBG: Verhandelingen van het Koninklijk Bataviaasch Genootschap van Kunsten en Wetenschappen.

Verh. KI: Verhandelingen van het Koninklijk Instituut voor Taal-, Land- en Volkenkunde.

C H A P T E R   O N E
INTRODUCTION

Purpose and Organization of the Study

Much has been written about Javanese kingship. Its magico-religious aspect has been of particular interest to several prominent Dutch scholars (Berg, Stutterheim, Bosch). Other writers have been concerned with state-administration (Rouffaer, Winter) and others with judicature (Soeripto, Jonker). Historical developments have also been the subject of much study by Krom, Berg, Hoesein Djajadiningrat and de Casparis, and general descriptions of Java and its people are to be found in the monumental works of Raffles, Veth and also in Pigeaud's latest work on Java in the 14th century. The sociological aspect of kingship is the subject of many of the writings of Wertheim and also of some of Burger's studies. A noted sociologist, Professor B. Schrieke, wrote on kingship in early Java, dealing with all aspects of state-life. His work, much to our regret, was left unfinished by the author's death.[1]

The purpose of this study is to examine kingship in the Later Mataram Period (16th through the 19th century) and is greatly inspired by Professor Schrieke's integrated approach to the subject. It attempts to present a survey in which the most relevant factors in state-life are seen in their proper relationships; each factor is studied from the point of view of its importance to the functioning of the state, its place in state organization and its interaction with the other factors surveyed. Since the emphasis here is on relationships, the investigation of the individual factors need not be exhaustively inclusive or minutely detailed. Such an

---

1 For the works of some of the authors mentioned, see the bibliography.

integrated approach is necessary, because the monarch so thoroughly dominated all aspects of state-life[2] that one cannot study the factors of kingship — authority, administration and finance — separately without risking serious distortions of perspective.

Because of the central and dominating position of the king, the study will begin with an analysis of the basic problem in state-life of the Later Mataram Period: namely, how the king could justify and make acceptable his dominating power. This is the problem of authority. We will have to probe into the interpretation and use of the magico-religious concepts which were the primary means of implementing the king's authority and of asserting and preserving the integrity of the state. In monarchies of extremely sacrosanct character, as were the Javanese kingdoms, magico-reli-gious concepts play the crucial role not only in justifying and strengthening the power of the monarch but also in explaining the roles of ruler and ruled as well as the relationship between the king and his subjects.

The second problem to study is the manner in which authority was applied to practical matters and what tools the kings had to achieve their ends. We come, then, to two other implementations of kingship: a technical one, namely royal administration; and a material one, the king's wealth, or in more general terms, the financing of the state. These two determinants of state-life, of course, must be seen as mere implementations of the king's rule; that is to say, they were operated only for and on behalf of the king. State-administration was an extension of kingly authority. Consequently, acquisition of wealth by the state, an important part of which was manual labor, had as its main purpose enhancing the authority of the king, and thus the grandeur of the state. Chapter II of this study tries to analyze the motives of state organization with the position of the king as the central theme.

An introductory discussion will be helpful in seeing the scope and outline of this study. We know that one's idea of state organization is based on the necessity of establishing a certain order in his communal life.[3] In

---

2   The tenability of this premise will be discussed below.
3   See further: William F. Ogburn and Meyer F. Nimkoff, *A Handbook of Sociology*, London, 1953, pp. 430-432; K. A. H. Hidding, *Gebruiken en Godsdiensten der Soendaneezen*, Batavia, 1930, pp. 14-19.

this respect, the Javanese of olden times must have been impressed by the pattern of regularity which dominates nature.[4] The coming and going of the seasons, the perpetual change between night and day, the cycles of life itself, the invariable trinity of birth, growth and death must have convinced him that the safest way to live is to attune himself to this cosmic order. This leads to an attitude of conservative traditionalism, a clinging to established customs and so to a distaste for change or for whatever may disturb the regular and predictable flow of events. In attuning himself to the Great Order man is led to accept the concept of Harmony, a cosmic harmony, in which everyone and everything has its ascribed place.[5] There is no room for a voluntary and mutual adjustment or a fine conciliation and conformation; rather, the universe is ordered by hard and stern rules. Deviation from them would set off a chain of reactions which might reach calamitous proportions. From here to a belief in the working of fate is but a very short distance. Harmony as a compelling need must therefore form the central concept in man's efforts toward organization. It is a harmony not only of man's world, the micro-cosmos, with the greater macro-cosmos, but also a harmony within his own sphere of life.

The Javanese, therefore, would not consider the state to have fulfilled its obligations if it did not encourage an inner psychological order (*tentrem*, peace and tranquillity of heart) as well as enforcing the formal order (*tata*). Only then is the state of perfect balance, of perfect harmony, achieved. These two goals form the cardinal points on which man's organizational activities shall be focused.

One such activity is religious practice: the worship of the gods with all its rules and ceremonies as well as all necessary material paraphernalia, most importantly religious structures and institutions. All of these must be seen as the efforts of man to lay a bridge of attunement between the world of man and the world of the gods. The activities of man within and thus towards the society in which he lives are mainly directed to maintaining this harmony within his sphere of life. He must take preventive and repressive measures against all possible disturbances of his social order and, because of the assumed mutual dependency

---

4   See p. 37 of this study for further discussion of this point.
5   See also: William James, *The Varieties of Religious Experience*, New York, 1961, p. 367.

between micro — and macro-cosmos, of the universal order also. In this sense social organization is not involvement in the members' daily routine but in maintaining adherence to established social patterns, the main manifestation of harmony, So its agencies primarily enforce such adherence, guarding against possible deviations and erasing whatever damage has been done, by magico-religious means as well as with penal measures of a physical character.

Following this line of reasoning, one can understand why state-administration in the kingdoms of old seems to have neglected people's needs, seems to have been detached from the toils of the common people. In agrarian countries where man's life depends so much more on the steady flow of seasonal change, where the concept of harmony is viewed more in terms of regularity and familiarity with the pattern of community life, any interference in the life of society may disturb the balance of the universe. Thus, the state will, as much as possible, refrain from such interference. Such restraint is feasible too because agrarian life, relatively, does not need much state-stimulus to work. Furthermore the narrow "espace-social" of the village does not create many needs which it cannot itself satisfy. It follows that progress in the modern sense of deliberate development and active stimulation could not have been considered a goal of the state. The role of the king is then more that of a protector than a developer.[6]

What is the position of the king in this inevitable relationship between the two cosmic orders? The state was the institution in which the king maintained dominance over all persons and goods. It is not very surprising, therefore, that the state should have been seen as an image of the Great Cosmic Order, in which the gods maintain absolute dominion. This schematic similarity between cosmic order and the state is seen as identity, and this serves a double purpose. First, as has been explained, if they are identical, the safety of the one assures the safety of the other. Second, and politically the most important, it serves to establish the king's power over his subjects. Similarity in form of substance tends to imply identity in character or quality. This is a train of thought which is familiar to simple correlative thinking. Thus, the state as a replica of the cosmic order must also have the propensies and capacities of that higher

---

6   See Chapter II, pp. 35ff and 39ff, for further discussion of this point.

order, a power which, as a part of the Great Order, no subject people dare restrict or disturb. This belief accounts for the absolute character of the old kingdoms. At the center and pinnacle of this organizational structure is the monarch.

The central and dominating position of the head of state can be explained in two ways according to the answer given to two questions. First, does man reconstruct the realm of the gods, with its highest divinity, in the image of the organizational structure of his own communal life where, via the concept of the *primus inter pares,* he arrives at the notion of a head of state with a craving for absolute power over his fellow beings? In so doing he would then justify this act of domination. Or, secondly, does the concept of the highest divinity as the ultimate source of the whole universe come from man's need for an explanation of all the phenomena in his visual as well as emotional world? And, by projecting an Almighty God, does he feel justified to ordain the king as the center of the micro-cosmos of man, as the bearer of absolute power over his worldly realm? Whatever the answer may be, the concept of the king as the center of the state from whom all power and authority emanate, around whom all activities of the state are concentrated, is then perfectly in harmony with the organizational structure of the rule of the universe, at least as man thought it to be.

Because of the central position of the king the whole apparatus of administration was inevitably an extension of the king's rule. Whatever power his administrators might have was derived from above.

Another factor important in defining state-life is the people who, economically speaking, form the most essential element. In a pre-mechanized world, they provide the power necessary for the production of wealth as well as for the defense of the realm. They are the source of physical force in times of peace as well as in times of war. So the relationship between the king and the people or between the ruler and the ruled, especially where the ruler has absolute power, depends upon what securities the people have against arbitrary acts of their monarch.[7]

A powerful check is, of course, rebellion. However, in a self-sufficient agrarian economy where the people can live from the produce of their

---

7   See p. 73 ff for a discussion of this point.

land and where communications have not been sufficiently developed to attract a subject from his life in his village, it is not very easy to raise a general uprising. Rebellion occurs only when the king's reign becomes so oppressive or so weak and careless that the people cannot fulfill their simple needs of life. The stability of state-life is more likely to be menaced by the many internal disturbances of wars, feuds, and dynastic conflicts. These are merely struggles for power between individuals and thus actually not the concern of the people; but, of course, the people are not excluded from participation. As the necessary suppliers of manpower and food and because they need the protection of their respective lords, they do become involved, especially when they live near the centers of power or near communication lines between the territories, whether it be road or river. To protect themselves from too much involvement in all these hostilities or too much oppression, people have developed effective devices of lesser resistance; they "disappear" into the woods or hills and wait until matters have settled a bit, or they migrate to a more remote and inaccessible place or to another realm entirely, where they can receive the protection of a greater lord who can assure them of a more peaceful life.

In this study, we try to examine both the theory and practice of kingship. It is evident that a study of the theory of kingship will put its stress on political thought, which, in a society where belief and religion play an important role, is closely connected with magico-religious concepts. Javanese texts on morals and manners, therefore, form a major source for this study. The practice of kingship will be studied mainly on the basis of historical evidence.

The study may be thought to cover too long a time-span, namely, from the reign of the first Mataram potentate, Panembahan Senapati, around 1585 in an unbroken, although split, dynastic-line down to the present. However, dealing with almost four centuries of history has this advantage: the vast array of facts and data offers a wider basis upon which to draw justifiable generalizations and conclusions. Moreover, common factors of place and religion — the same geographical location (the region south of Mount Merapi) and the prevalence of Islam throughout the period — make it convenient to study the Later Mataram Period as a whole.

Moreover, as will be made evident in the following chapters, during these four hundred years no basic changes seem to have taken place in the structural organization of the Mataram state, nor in the ideological bases of state-life. However, an historical approach presupposes a concept of change in society, be it slow and almost imperceptible or of a sweeping dynamism. Awareness of the possibility of change has to be especially sharpened when studying such a traditional society as Java because its apparent traditionalism tends to obscure factors of change. In the case of Mataram two main causes of change have to be taken into account: Islam and the existence of the power of V.O.C. (the Dutch East-India Company), at first side by side, and later superior to the kingdom of Mataram.

Islam initiated changes in Mataram state-life only in the apparent influence of Muslim *walis* on the policies of rulers, but this influence did not continue beyond the reign of Sunan Amangkurat II (1677-1703). Afterwards, Islam gave new impetus to resistance towards foreign rule with the idea of the *perang sabil* (holy war). However, we shall see that there is no real evidence to prove that this idea had great or widespread influence at least in official state-life although, amongst the populace, Islam remained the great moving force against any political oppression.[8] The limited-ness of the *perang sabil*'s influence can perhaps be attributed to the fact that the Kingdoms of Later Mataram had never been as thoroughly Islamized as the sultanates of Acheh and Malacca; Old-Javanese elements remained most influential in state-life.

The effect of Dutch power in Java was quite different from that of Islam. Its steadily increasing involvement in the internal affairs of Mataram and moreover its steadily expanding control of the political situation in Java as a whole nibbled away at the king's ultimate authority. It cannot be denied that on many occasions it was the V.O.C. and later the Netherland-Indies Government which upheld and restored the king's position as head of state, with due remuneration. However, the ever-shrinking boundaries of Mataram (due to loss of territory to the Dutch) and the consequent loss of wealth made it very difficult for the Mataram mon-archs to sustain the policy of aggrandizement — a policy which was at the crux of state-craft of those times. Moreover, and perhaps more importantly, loss of territory resulted in loss of revenues to finance the administration of the state. Revenue came primarily from the *lungguh* salary-system, which made control of land by the monarch a necessity; and the infiltrating money-

---

8   See p. 80 ff for further discussion of this point.

economy in the more recent times did not help to solve these complex problems.

One is justified in believing, therefore, that the Mataram state, and increasingly so from the reign of Sunan Amangkurat II, had undergone a somewhat stunted development with a touch of artificiality which made it impossible for Mataram to develop towards such an uninhibited, imperial confidence as that of its ideal, Madjapahit, or even, perhaps, towards its own complete destruction.

These impeding factors, particularly as they were backed by an effective military force of the Dutch, succeeded in implanting a feeling of impotence which subsequently led to an attitude of resignation. In the writings of the two royal literati of the 19th century, the ruler of Surakarta, Paku Buwana IX (1861-1893), and the head of the Mangkunegaran House, Mangkunegara IV (1853-1881), we can detect a tone of contemplative appeasement and submission to fate quite different from the *élan vital* we find in the narration of Sultan Agung's deeds in the *Babad Tanah Djawi* or even in the attitude of the Dutch themselves who described this monarch in terms revealing the authority and prestige of that ruler.[9]

These changes notwithstanding, ideas about state and state-policy did not undergo important changes. The challenge of political as well as economic change was not met with changing ideas about state-life. Moreover, as will be made evident in the following chapters, during these four hundred years no basic changes are to be detected in the structural organization of the Mataram state, nor in the ideological concept of state-life. Although Islam, and much more so, the intrusions of the Dutch East India Company (V.O.C.) and later of the Netherland-Indies Government formed a real challenge towards change to the Javanese kingdoms, there was no adequate reaction. Clinging to tradition, Mataram made only inadequate modifications or piecemeal adjustments, undoubtedly also due to its limited means and very much reduced authority; for, after the Gianti-pact of 1755 and the Peace of Salatiga of 1757, Mataram had fallen apart into four small principalities, Surakarta, Jogjakarta, the Mangkunegaran and the Pakualaman. Although formally retaining their status as the independent *Vorstenlanden* (Lands of the Kings — the official

---

9 See p. 49.

name given by the Netherland-Indies Government), the principalities were bound by contract to the suzerain. They were, in actual practice, no more than provinces of the Netherland East-Indies, although receiving perhaps fewer benefits than was bestowed on the "directly governed territories ."

Mataram's adherence to traditional concepts, or in other words, the relatively static attitude towards state-life which characterizes the period, enables us to look for general trends and tendencies and detect a pattern in the ideas and practices of the state and thus come to an integrated study of this Later Mataram Kingdom, the intention of this study.

Sources

To the knowledge of this writer, there are two Dutch scholars who have devoted considerable efforts to the study of the Later Mataram period as an historical entity. They are Professor H. J. de Graaf and the late Professor B. Schrieke, a sociologist. The former, an historian, has written a book on the history of Indonesia,[10] the most laudable feature of which is that the writer gives it a "human touch" by relating events of every-day life and giving much space to first-hand accounts of conditions in a certain place or time in Indonesian history which are very illustrative for the correct evaluation and understanding of the course of historical events. Moreover, de Graaf took up the task of writing about the important figures and events in the history of Later Mataram.[11] His work is valuable from the point of view of historiographic documentation. One might have liked, however, to see more interpretation in these studies.

Professor Schrieke's major work on kingship in Java,[12] which includes a study of the whole "Moslem Mataram" period, clearly reveals the fact that it was left incomplete at the death of this prominent scholar. Some subjects were treated only cursorily, while others — for instance, the question of the king's position and especially of his realm — are dealt

---

10 H. J. de Graaf, *Geschiedenis van Indonesië*, 's-Gravenhage, 1949.
11 H. J. de Graaf, "De Regering van Panembahan Senapati Ingalaga," "De Regering van Sultan Agung, Vorst van Mataram," "De Regering van Sunan Mangku-rat I, Vorst van Mataram," in *Verh. KI*, 13, 23 and 33.
12 B. Schrieke, *Indonesian Sociological Studies*, vol. II, The Hague, 1957.

with at considerable length. Schrieke also succeeded in determining the inner territories of Madjapahit and the regions of Later Mataram, and, in addition, he paid a good deal of attention to state-administration, particularly that of Mataram. Professor Schrieke's book, even in this unfinished form, is most valuable to the knowledge of Java's cultural history, primarily because it attempts to present political life in Java in one integrated study. It covers a period extending from Airlangga's time (1019-1049) to "Muslim Mataram" (1575-present), truly a very long time-span of approximately ten centuries; the justification for this lay in his observation that, after each dynastic break,the new king always considered himself not an initiator of a new regime but as the perpetuator of the old order, "at any rate in appearance." So Javanese history was seen as a unified continuity and more recent history can make a contribution toward an understanding of a more remote past.[13] Most certainly this study is a very detailed and careful piece of work which has done much in leading the way towards a better appraisal of Java's cultural history. Not much has been written on this subject that displays such an approach of coordination and unification of historical data. It has formed a most important directive to this study.

As far as sources and material for this thesis is concerned, major use has been made of Javanese writings from the period concerned. Contemporary ideas and customary practices have also been referred to, always with care and always taking into consideration the possibility of change in the course of time. Analogy and comparison with similar circumstances and similar practices of other periods in Indonesian history or of other places should form an incessant check. As for the written Javanese sources, although ample material is available, these writings are regrettably very unevenly spread over the period as well as over the subjects to be treated. For instance, the question of the king's position, the ideals of kingship and *prijaji*-ship, their virtues and vices, are treated in several writings at length. "Histories" (*Babad*'s) have to be sorted very carefully (although not with such a degree of suspicious caution as Professor Berg displays), and one must ask whether they are based on facts or whether they are deliberately or inadvertently falsified, Not much can be found about state-administration

---

13 *Ibid.*, p. 4.

and the financial problems of the state except whatever can be extracted from the position and interrelations of office-holders mentioned in the "Histories." Beginning only with the 19th century was codification of legal concepts considered necessary especially to facilitate relations with the Nether-land-Indies Government, its functionaries or its subjects. These codes afford material on state-administration and state-finance. The Dutch scholars' and officials' growing interest in all aspects of Javanese society also stimulated such efforts towards codification. The recentness of these sources does not, however, form an unsurpassable hindrance to reconstructing state-life in Mataram because, here again, adherence to tradition formed a barrier to great changes, and innovations and adjustments to more modern needs usually are easy to detect in these sources.[14]

Categories of Javanese sources used are:

1. The *pakem*-literature, the repertory of the *wajang*, the Javanese puppet-play. Each *lakon* or play is constructed according to a fixed pattern; only the stories are different. *Pakems* merely outline the story, and thus it is only from a performance that one can appreciate that the *wajang* is "*the* mirror" of Javanese life. The *dalang* (puppeteer), within the frame of the *lakon* and within the boundaries of technical as well as ritualistic limitations, has surprisingly great freedom to give to the performance the necessary ornamentation and allusions which enhances its appeal for the contemporary audience. The fact has to be borne in mind that the *lakon* performed is mostly chosen to suit the needs of the moment, may it be a simple family affair like a wedding or a birth, or the interest of a community, usually the *desa* (village) or even the state, and this because of the suggestive, magical character of a *wajang*-performance. The *wajang lakon* paints a picture not only of an idealized state-life, but of state-policy and practice as well. The Hindu accent of the stories need not discourage their use as source material because they have become thoroughly assimilated by acceptance or modification and also by considerable addition to the repertory with new, invented *lakons*.

---

14 See pp. 51-52.

2. The *babad*-literature, the "histories," relate events and happenings of the past. Some are centered around and actually written for the benefit of a certain court or dynasty and may be considered of a "national" character in the sense that they are concerned with the whole kingdom as, for example, the *Babad Tanah Djawi* (written from the middle of the 16th century on), the *Babad Mataram* (last half of the 18th century), and the *Serat Konda*. Others are of a local character, such as the *Babad Patjina* and the *Babad Dipanegara* (first half of the 19th century). According to Professor Berg, the main purpose of a *babad*'s "literary magic" was to enhance the august and sacral importance of the king or the ruling potentate. The choice of subjects and the organization of the book is dedicated to the achievement of this goal, making it less than reliable, although not wholly unusable, as historical source material, particularly for the periods of the earlier past. The necessity for magically correct interpretation justified the *pudjangga*, the priestly court-writer, in indulging himself with omissions or distortions of events of the past.[15] However, the first compiler of the Later Mataram *babads* may have made absurd mistakes in the recounting of the periods before the emergence of the Kingdom of Demak simply because he was ill-informed. Documented material may have been lost or destroyed when the successive kingdoms after Madjapahit changed location or religion. The Mataram *pudjangga* had, then, to write a new compilation with material handed on by oral narration.

As source material for this study, these *babads* do not offer very much clear, unequivocal information, but they do reveal the general political situation of the time, especially the power relations between the different parts of the realm or the different power-holders; indeed, they mainly relate conflicts between holders of power. State policy towards the welfare of the population can scarcely be detected. It is important to observe that there is considerable "lend-lease" of material between *babads*.

15 See C. C. Berg, "Javaansche Geschiedschrijving," in F. W. Stapel, *Geschiedenis van Nederlandsch Indië*, part II, Amsterdam, 1938.

3. Another group of sources are the *piwulangs* (instruction). Under this category the Javanese place a large assortment of writings of which the main characteristic is that they give some or other kind of instruction, mostly of a moralistic character. They are not written in story form, although they may contain illustrative short tales often about persons of virtue from *wajang* literature or from history. These writings may have been lifted out of a larger text and presented separately because of their instructional merits. Such a *piwulang* is the *Asta Brata* taken from the *Serat Rama* (± 1750), the Javanese version of the famous Indian epic, *Ramayana*, and meant as an instruction in the kingly attitude. *Piwulangs* were written in poetic metre and were to be sung at intimate gatherings. There are those intended for young people, for women, office-holders, soldiers and those for man in general. Paku Buwana IX (1861-1893) and Mangkune-gara IV (1853-1881) personally contributed much to this kind of literature, and *piwulang* composing was a part of gentlemanly education and leisure. Older *piwulangs*, like the *Nitisruti*, an adaptation of an originally Indian text, exist too. The underlying religious basis of these moral poems may be Hinduistic or Islamic or both. For our purpose, *piwulangs* reveal clearly Javanese ideals as to the concept of the ideal man, woman, king or official, and from the last two we can draw conclusions as to what are the attributes of a just and expedient rule.

Not only *piwulangs* but almost all writings, even those in story form, had a didactic purpose; words have magic power and the mere reading of a text bestows beneficial or, if one is unauthorized, destructive influence. Thus, the meticulous detailing of the various *wewaler* (taboos) of the rulers of Mataram in the *Babad Tanah Djawi*[16] was undoubtedly meant to be carefully heeded by their descendants, and in the *Wulangreh* of Paku Buwana IV (1788-1820) these taboos were summed up again. The story of Kodja Djadjahan, with its Islamic character, relates the virtues of the grandvizier Kodja Djadjahan and is meant to be held up as a mirror for high officials.[17]

---

16 *Babad Tanah Djawi*, ed. Meinsma, 's-Gravenhage, 1941, pp. 57,104.
17 R. M. Ng. Poerbatjaraka, *Kapustakan Djawi*, Djakarta, 1952, p. 96.

4. Javanese state-ordinances and decisions of the king and high dignitaries. These official decrees, called *angger* (statute or regulation) or *piagem* (decisions), were, as is explained above, all of recent date, which does not mean that they were of recent invention. One can be fairly certain, by checking them against *babad* and other Javanese writings, that these decrees reflect age-old state practice.[18] The study of state administration and taxation is reconstructed mainly from these materials.

Use has also been made of material found in the narratives of foreigners, usually Dutch envoys and military commanders, and accounts of the V.O.C. as additional material to supplement hiatuses, but more importantly as valuable means of comparison.

An account of source material for this study of course cannot be ended without mentioning the studies of the prominent scholars, preponderantly Dutch, which describe, analyze and interpret Java's tradition. Krom, Brandes, van Vollenhoven as well as Berg, Schrieke, Stutterheim, Bosch, Pigeaud, Wertheim, Hooykaas, van Leur, ter Haar and recently de Casparis and — among Indonesians — Hoesein Djajadiningrat, Poerbatjaraka, Soepomo and Yamin are but a few of the great number of men of science who have given their best efforts to this particular field of study.

---

18 See p. 71.

C H A P T E R   T W O
MAGICAL AND RELIGIOUS IMPLEMENTATION
OF KINGSHIP:
THE PROBLEM OF AUTHORITY

The King and His People: The Kawula-Gusti Relationship

If we see the state as a social institution, where men through combined effort try to achieve certain goals, and in so doing have to make use of a certain amount of organization and coordination, then we must take into account the two important human elements of organization, the organizer and the organized, the leader and the follower, or, in the traditional Javanese terms, the ruler and his subject, *kawula-gusti* (servant [and] master).[1] In Javanese traditional life the rela-tionship between servant and master is not impersonal; it is rather a personal and close tie of mutual respect and responsibility. Ideally, it is modeled after the care and love of family ties. This was also true in social communication in general. Such an attitude is revealed by the fact that the Javanese frequently address a stranger with the title *ki-sanak* or *saderek*, both words meaning "relative," in general. And the common saying, *tuna satak bati sanak* (a loss of some money [but] a gain of a kin), indicates that even in the accepted mercenary character of trade a loss of profit is considered worthwhile if one can instead gain a kin.

It could be argued, though, that social values cannot be judged in terms of words and maxims only, as they do not always reveal the underlying

---

1 Old Javanese: *kawula, bhrtya* — bondsman, retainer (Th. G. Th. Pigeaud, *Java in the 14th Century*, Vol. V, The Hague, 1962. In modern Javanese it has a broader meaning: subject in general. Old Jav.: *gusti* — yeoman, master; in modern Jav. the meaning of "the king" and "the lord God" is included.

motivations of the speaker and furthermore through customary use, or better, abuse, they have become empty phrases devoid of social reality. But if we consider the *kawula-gusti* concept in its mystical garb we can see clearly how genuinely deep-rooted this sense of close interrelation is in the Javanese mind. Although mysticism is considered *wadi* (dangerously secret) and is thought available only to the selected few, it was and is still immensely popular with all strata of the population,and any respectable Javanese must at least know something about the so-called *ngelmu* (the sacred knowledge) of which mysticism forms a dominant part.

In Javanese mysticism, the words *djumbuhing kawula gusti* (the merging of servant and master)[2] describe the highest goal of man's life, namely the achievement of the ultimate "one-ness" (*manunggal*) with God. This is the more dramatic since the words *Kawula* and *gusti* denote the very lowest and the very highest status of man in society. However, and this is important to our argument, unity of servant and master is possible only because there are certain ties between and properties common to man and God. These properties lie within the most indescribable essence or substance of God and man which the Javanese denote with the word *suksma* (soul), of Indian origin, or with the word *nur* (light), derived from the Arabic. Since all men possess these properties, one can understand how decisive close- and personal relations are in determining social communication in Javanese society, bridging even the wide gaps of rank and blood. However, despite the common bond, neither servant nor master is allowed to transgress the formal dividing lines of the social hierarchy, apparent in birth or rank and perceptible in the many rules governing the etiquette of wearing apparel, use of language (*krama-inggil*, *krama*, *madya* and *ngoko*), the use of color or the paying of homage. In other words, deep concern about each others' needs and sorrows or an intense feeling of sympathy towards each other cannot justify forgetting one's place in society, a place which fate has allotted. Thus the Javanese commitment to the *kawula-gusti* concept makes social communication a fine and intricate art in itself because one must be careful to keep one's place while maintaining a familial concern towards another.

---

2   In the *Wulangreh* of Paku Buwana IV (1788-1820) the idea is expressed as *pamoring gusti kawula*. Paku Buwana IV, *Wulangreh*, Kediri, 1929, p. 35.

The *kawula-gusti* concept is deeply colored with another characteristic of Javanese thinking: an unshakable belief in fate, in things preordained, expressed in the words *pinesti* (determined), *tinitah* (ordained), or the Arabic loanword *tekdir* (predestined). There were two main strata of Javanese society, the *wong tjilik*, the common man, and the *penggede*, the ruling class, not so much in terms of economic wealth or superiority of blood, but more in terms of servitude and masterdom, that of *kawula* (servant) vis à vis *bendara* (master), and one's place in this social order and thus one's rights and duties were believed to be predestined, a belief which unquestionably contributed much towards the smooth operation of social functions. The Javanese belief does not seem to be *directly* related to the Indian principle of *Karman*, for evidence of the Indian formulation is scarce in writings of the Later Mataram period.[3] This is not remarkable since the belief in the inevitability of things is expressed in the God-ordained *tekdir* of Islam, which by then had sent its roots deep into Javanese soil.[4] That fate is capricious is stressed repeatedly in stories and *piwulangs* and serves to explain away, to obliterate and erase possible social or political tensions in events in history. The story of Djaka Tingkir and that of Ki Ageng Pemanahan from the *Babad Tanah Djawi* will serve as an example. Djaka Tingkir, destined to become the king of Padjang, when still a young man lived with Ki Ageng Sela. The wise man saw the sure sign of royalty, a radiant light, emanate from the sleeping Djaka Tingkir. This very much saddened Ki Ageng Sela, because he had spent a life of fervent prayer and rigorous asceticism, hoping to obtain God's favor so that he himself would father a line of kings. However, in order to save what he thought to be his right, he asked Djaka Tingkir to allow him to "continue" his luck. The youth agreed. So, later, his hope became reality but through the unpredictable working of fate; his grandson, Ki Ageng Pemanahan, seemingly by accident, came to

---

3 That it was known to the Javanese of the time can be seen in the "Serat Tjabolang." Th. Pigeaud, "De Serat Tjabolang en de Serat Tjentini. Inhoudsopgaven," in *VBG*, Vol. LXXII, part II, 1933, p. 35.

4 Apparently, instead of the inevitability of re-incarnation, the Javanese strongly believe in a strict and divine law of reward and reprisal for deeds done which will befall the person concerned in his present life, or, and this is more important for Javanese morality, which will affect the lives of his close kin or descendants. See also Mangkunegara IV, *Dwidja Isjwara*, ed. Padmasusastra, Surakarta, 1899, p. 43.

drink the coconut-juice which a certain Ki Ageng Giring had left behind in order to be able to savour it after a day's hard work. Drinking this coconut juice, however, was the necessary prerequisite — as Ki Ageng Giring had been told by "a voice" in the coconut — to one's descendants ever ruling Java.[5]

On the political scene, the domination of Mataram over the mighty princes of East Java and even over the priestly domain of Giri had been predestined and duly explained long before by the then ruling Sunan Giri. Undoubtedly this prediction served as a means of making the rulers of Surabaja comply with their fate. Nevertheless, Surabaja took up arms against its suzerain again and again; the heaviest fighting, according to the *Babad Tanah Djawi*, occurred during the reign of Amangkurat II (1677-1703), when the *adipati* of Surabaja, *tumenggung* Djajapuspita, defended himself against the attacks of the combined Mataram and Dutch troops for over ten months because of his faith in Islam. But finally Djajapuspita had to leave his fortified town in defeat when he began to hesitate and lose his faith and, finally, ask the help of the Balinese.[6]

Setting aside the question of historical correctness of the narrative as not relevant in this connection, these tales insist that fate and not Mataram had weakened the power of Djajapuspita's troops so that they could be overpowered. Therefore, fate and not its own accomplishments made Mataram ruler over East Java. Thus, acts and situations were made legitimate or at least were justified because of their unavoidability.

Still another and a much more striking example of the rigidity of destiny is found in the repertory of the *wajang*, the Javanese shadow-play, namely in the story (*lakon*) Bratajuda, the war between the Pandawas and the Korawas. The Pandawas' envoy, Sri Betara Kresna, was so enraged by the insulting attitude of the Korawas that he took on his *tiwikrama*-form as a huge thousand-headed and thousand-limbed giant. He could have crushed the Korawas and even the entire population of Ngastina at that very moment, if the god Surya, Suralaja's messenger, had not reminded him that destiny had to work out its course, that the fearful and destructive Bratajuda had to be fought and that the fate of the Korawas was that they

---

5 *Babad Tanah Djawi*, pp. 36, 65, 67.
6 *Babad Tanah Djawi*, pp. 68, 322.

would perish in it. Here even a deity (Kresna is an incarnation of the god Wisnu) was not permitted to change the course of fate.[7]

In explaining the working of destiny, one seemingly inconsistent fact has to be pointed out in the story about Ki Djaka Tingkir. Ki Ageng Sela's desire that his descendants be allowed to continue Djaka Tingkir's reign actually did come true when his great-grandson Panembahan Senapati founded the kingdom of Mataram towards the end of the sixteenth century, thus giving proof that coming events can be influenced by man's actions. Such inconsistency is, however, explained by the law of reward and reprisal. Ki Ageng Sela's wish was fulfilled only because of his *semedi*,[8] the consistent concentration of his whole being on the goal he expected to reach. The performance of a *semedi* releases powers, in Javanese thought conceived of as a "wave of heat"[9] which steadily increases in intensity according to the degree of perseverance in the execution of the *semedi* and eventually is felt as a disturbance in nature. Such reciprocity of action between the micro-cosmos of man and the macro-cosmos of the gods is traditionally illustrated by the *gara-gara*-scene in the *wajang*-play, when the hero's ardent *semedi*," because of his distress or because of his wish to attain a certain goal, results in a disturbance in nature which, in turn, brings the hero's wishes to the attention of the gods. Only the consent of the gods, or at least their interference, will restore nature to its normal order. *Sing sapa gede panjuwune, bakal katekan sedyane*, "he who prays fervently will have his wishes fulfilled," is therefore thought to be an unfailing truth, although the result might not necessarily be immediate.

This sense of an exact rendering of reward or punishment is so strong that it is thought that an ardent wish even for. an evil end when strengthened by abstention and self-chastisement will be rewarded, but by the demonic goddess Durga, the female counterpart of Batara Kala, the evil aspect of the god Guru (Ciwa). However, fulfillment of such a wish, because of its ill intent, can be only temporary. Moreover, eventually it will be fatal and disastrous to the person concerned.[10] Illustrations are to

---

7   Jasadipoera, Kyai (ed. Cohen-Stuart), "Serat Bratayuda," *VBG*,Vol. XXVIII (1860), pp. 15, 16.

8   *Semedi* is the yogic technique of establishing contact between man and God.

9   *Babad Tanah Djawi*, p. 77. Because of Panembahan Senapati's ascetic practice, the Ocean's "waters became as hot as boiling water."

10 K. G. P. A. A. Mangkunegara VII, *On the Wayang Kulit (Purwa) and Its Symbolic and Mystical Elements*, trans. Claire Holt, Southeast Asia Program Data Paper No. 27, Cornell University,

be found in many of the stories of the *wajang*. For instance, in the *lakon* Bradjadenta-Bradjamusti, the giant Bradjadenta buys Batari Durga's help (black magic) at the cost of his own death at the hands of his nephew, Gatutkatja, knight of Pringgadani.[11] Perhaps the belief in, if not human, then unfailing divine justice is reflected in the notion that undeserved wealth acquired through the help of the spirit Njai Blorong, a beautiful snake-bodied woman with scales of gold, must always end in untimely death to serve as her slave forever after; it is also thought that such wealth demands the sacrifice of one's child who will encounter a serious and long-lasting mishap, That such justice is perceived by the Javanese in the even stronger sense of a self-executing natural law is markedly expressed in the word *kewales*. *Kewales* denotes the working of repercussion, automatically, without specification of an agent of action, for the prefix *ke-* is used in this verb form.

Apart from obtaining favors from the Gods, which is the most popular notion of the purpose of *semedi*, there is a more basic, a deeper purpose to obtain knowledge of God's will or, more vulgarly, to see into the future. In the language of the *Babad Tanah Djawi* this is described as *neges karsaning hyang ingkang murbeng pandulu* (trying to understand the will of the all-seeing), or, more frequently, as *maneges karsaning Pangeran* (trying to understand God's will)[12] . The will of God is almost never disclosed in clear, unequivocal terms but rather in a veiled and intricately indirect form, available to all but comprehensible to only those worthy of such an exceptionally high and therefore "dangerous" favor. Indirect forms of information, such *pralambang* or *pasemon* ("covered information") given in perceptible form or in words, are frequently used, even essential in social communication. So *pralambangs* are not used in the communication between Creator and created only, but also, and very extensively, between man and man, where crude directness is avoided as much as possible and veiled and subtle insinuation is preferred. The expression "a kick for a slave, an insinuation for a lower official, a smile for a high dignitary" (*dupak budjang, semu mantri, esem bupati*) indicates that a rude reprimand is fit only for the lowest and that a *bupati* (a high

---

Ithaca, N.Y., 1957, p. 13 (original in *Djawa*, Vol. XIII, 1933).

11 J. Kats, *Het Javaansche Toneel*, Vol. I, Batavia 1923 p. 294.

12 *Babad Tanah Djawi*, p. 245.

dignitary, regent) has to be careful in interpreting the intentions of his lord.

A *pralambang* from the time of the fall of the Dutch in 1942 under the attacks of the Japanese forces will illustrate the interpretation of such "covered information." Some two or three years before, a traffic regulation required that a horse-drawn vehicle should have as a turn-signal a white disc wi a round red reflector in the center, mounted on a stick which the driver had to extend to indicate the direction he intended to take. The Javanese believed this was a divine sign that the Japanese would be masters over Java because the white disc with red dot looked exactly like the insignia of the Japanese "Navy O" fighters (a red ball painted on the gleaming white surface of the aeroplane), which were the first seen in Java's skies before the invasion. That this interpretation came *after* the Dutch surrendered did not in the least lessen the validity of the *pralambang*, for the Javanese knew that interpretation came late simply because nobody had had sense enough to read the "writing on the wall" earlier.

Semedi is seen as a means of bridging the gap between the unfathomable depths of God's knowledge and, in terms of time and clarity, the narrow and dim view of man. If man can perform *semedi*, there must be certain essential qualities which are common to both man and God. This does not make man God's equal but it does allow him to contact intimately, and finally merge with God. Thus it is possible for man to become one with his Creator, which is what *djumbuhing kawula-gusti* tries to explain.[13]

Returning again to the relations between ruler and ruled, the *kawula-gusti* concept does not merely refer to a relation-ship between the high and the low, but rather to a close interdependency between two distinct but nevertheless inseparable elements, two elements which ultimately form two aspects of the same thing. This syncretism is derived from Indian theology (e.g., Trimurti and Hari-hara). An early Javanese expression of the unity of disparate elements is the well-known statue of Krtanagara of Singhasari as Bhatara Ciwa-Buddha. True to all mysticism, these syncretic ideas seek to prove that all things are only aspects, *çakti's*, emanations, only integral parts of the all-embracing One, in Javanese thought personified in the god Sang Hyang Wenang (the Omnipotent), or more popularly in

---

13 See above, p. 15.

his son, Sang Hyang Tunggal (the One).

The Javanese, with their projective-imaginative thinking,[14] symbolized this *kawula-gusti* unity with a strikingly appropriate object, namely the *keris*, a formal dagger-type weapon. The two parts of the *keris*, the scabbard (*warangka*) and the blade (*tjuriga*), have been given a singularly mystical interpretation;[15] the scabbard is likened to the people and the blade to the king, thus describing a necessary relationship, the one incomplete without the presence of the other, and also an interdependency in the sense that the scabbard protects the blade from damage and conversely the blade protects the scabbard (which is usually made of the finest wood sheathed in ornately chiseled silver or gold) from theft and loss. The value of a *keris* is judged by the magical force, contained in the *pamor* (meteorite iron inlay on its blade) and derived from the magical power of its *empu* (weaponsmith). But since the blade symbolizes the king as the core, the essence, the guiding force of the state, it has to be worthy, according to

---

14 For the Javanese nothing is without meaning and consequently he is apt to search for meaning in acts, words or situations, however rationally incomprehensible or unimportant they may seem. Visible or perceptible things are thought to be possible projections of more abstract or concealed meanings, expressed in the word *surasa* (meaning, inner purpose). Analogies are therefore also very much used in explanations, and similarities or supposed similarities in form can lead to identification in sense or meaning, a train of thought which has led Professor C. C. Berg to his intricate and elaborate theory of dynastic change among the rulers of Java. (See C. C. Berg, "The Islamization of Java," in *Studia Islamica*, IV, Oct. 22, 1955, p. lllff., especially Par. III, IV). If the *pralambang* illustrates the interpretation of similarities or the projection of concealed meanings, the *kerata-basa*, a kind of folk etymology (see Ch. F. Hockett, *A Course in Modern Linguistics*, New York, 1958, p. 288), are, as explained by S. Padmosoekotjo, words "which are given a meaning taken from the constituting syllables or pronunciation-parts, by means of adaptation [of the sound in the syllables] to fit [the meaning given]." (S. Padmosoekotjo, *Ngengrengan Kasusastran Djawa*, Jogjakarta, 1958, Vol. I, p. 43.) Although *kerata-basa* is only a play of words, it does illustrate the highly imaginative and speculative working of Javanese projective-correlative thinking. The word *sruwal* for instance, meaning pair of pants, consists of the first syllable *sru-* which in *kerata-basa* is synchronized to fit to the word *saru* (shameful) and the second syllable *-wal* pointing to the fitting word *uwal* (not to adhere to, to loosen from) so that we derive the adapted meaning "it will be shameful if it ever comes loose," which it certainly would be if it ever happened! Even modern words are given a *kerata-basa* meaning. "Scooter" in Javanese pronounced as "sekuter"; the syllable *seku-*is adaptable to the word *sideku* (sitting with bent elbow as support), *-ter* synchronizes with *banter* (fast). The adapted meaning will be then: "sitting with bent elbow but acquiring a fast pace as well." The importance of word-play and word-interpretation to seek for a hidden meaning is sufficiently illustrated by the examples above.

15 In Javanese mysticism the *djumbuhing kawula-gusti* has been symbolically visualized by "the merging of the scabbard into the blade" (*warangka mandjing tjuriga*), the scabbard being man and the blade God, a reversed view of actuality, wherein the Javanese find great delight, especially to illustrate — in such paradoxes — the idea of the mystical "impossible possibilities." (See further: P. J. Zoetmulder, *Pantheisme en Monisme in de Javaansche Soeloek-litteratuur*, Nijmegen, 1935, pp. 236, 320ff.)

whatever standard, of its sheath. The indivisible link between ruler and subject is also compared to a ring (*sesupe*), the king as the *sesotya* (the precious stone) and the people as the *embanan* (the setting). From the prototype Indian *Nitiçastra*, with its point by point advice and instructive comparisons, is derived the analogy between the lion or tiger and the forest[16] and the king and his people. The mutual protection of lion and forest and king and people is not only beneficial but necessary to both parties. This analogy is found also in the Javanese *Panitisastra* of 1808, a translation of an older Old-Javanese version.[17]

Another source of information about the king-subject relationship is of course the *wajang*. Although its exact age has not yet been agreed upon, if one accepts Rassers' theory,[18] its origin can be placed far back in history. It can be shown to have existed at least in the eleventh century A.D. and thus long before the Later Mataram period. *Wajang* gives to everyone in the widely variegated audience attending such a play something to take advantage of; it is in one sense entertainment for all, but in a more important sense instruction for all, for in it are illustrated the multifarious aspects of human behavior, from the lowest greed to the highest morality, from the little weaknesses of men or gods to the undeniable strength of faith, from the intrigues of diplomacy to the stern working of fate, from

---

16 *Nitiçastra*, ed. R. M. Ng.Poerbatjaraka, trans. R. M. B. Djajahendra, Batavia, 1940, point 10. This comparison is also used in the very popular *Serat Rama*, when Rama-widjaja instructs his younger brother Barata in the art of ruling:
  "the whole populace can be likened to a forest and
      the king to a lion
  whose security lies in the denseness of the thicket.
  Should the forest ever become open
  the lion would lose his regard,
  and his strength would be of no use;
  if he struggles he soon will be overpowered.
  So it is agreed
  that a king should love his people
  like the tiger the woods."
  (K. Jasadipura, *Serat Rama*, Semarang, 1919,
  p. 43.)

17 From the point of view of continuity, it is noteworthy that the *Panitisastra*, as a reverence to Islam, is introduced with a couplet of homage to the Lord God and His Prophet, Kandjeng Nabi Mohammad, a tradition in Javanese-Islamic literature, which however is a continuation of a Hinduistic custom of beginning a literary work with a word of homage to the god Wisnu.
  R. M. Ng. Poerbatjaraka, *Kapustakan Djawi*, Djakarta, 1952, p. 142.

18 W. H. Rassers, *Pañji, the Culture Hero*, The Hague, 1959, pp. 98, 99. For the historical development of the *wajang* puppets see also: Th. Pigeaud, *Javaansche Volksvertoningen*, Batavia, 1938, p. 365ff.

witty pun to mystical dialogue. *Wajang* is thus an important source of information on contemporary social attitudes and more so since new *lakons* were continuously added to the repertory by court-sages who were skilled in grasping the mood of the time, or — and this is not a great exception — by the ruler himself, like the poet-prince Mangkunegara IV, whom one may expect knew the needs, views and ambitions of his time.[19] If we thereby take the sacrosanct character of the *wajang*-play into consideration, we can safely assume that the *wajang* actually reflects the ideals and aspirations of Javanese society. Therefore, the *wajang* as the reflection of Javanese ideals *par excellence* also tells us something about the ideal ruler-subject relationship.

In the Javanese shadow play, one can observe the existence of a group of characters quite distinct from the figures of the right and those of the left, following the well-known Javanese cosmological classification. The puppets of this third group are always pictured with physical deformities and of a ribald and somewhat uncouth disposition, and they are thought to represent — and to an extent symbolize — the common people. They are called *panakawan*, which does not only mean that they are servants (*abdi*) but also the inseparable companions and at times the mentors of their respective masters.

Of these, one group, Semar and his sons, (Nala)gareng, Petruk and, in Jogjakarta, Bagong, serve the right or "good" side. Togog and his companion Sarawita (or Bilung) serve the left or "bad" side. In the *wajang*-piay they actually are no more than jesters or jokers who give to the performance the much appreciated time to relax in laughter. However, one of the various interpretations about their place in the *wajang* gives them a more important role. Semar is actually no less than the deity Hyang Ismaja, the older brother of Hyang Manikmaja (more usually called Batara Guru), ruler of the celestial world and the universe. In the Sundanese-speaking area of Java, Togog (sometimes Tedjamantri in Sundanese) is thought of as the equally godly brother of Semar, named Hyang Tedja-maya, but to the Javanese he is the treacherous servant of the *buta* (giants), serving those who will pay the most.[20] To Semar and

---

19 See p. 48.

20 R. Hardjowirogo, *Sedjarah Wajang Purwa*, Djakarta, 1952, pp. 97, 98, 99, 100, 131, 132.

Togog fell the duty to be the guardians of mankind, respectively on the "good" and "bad" side. Still another interpretation identified Semar with the formlessness of eternity,while his sons Gareng, Bagong and Petruk are thought to personify the past, present and future.[21]

Such an identification of the most important *panakawans* with, on the one hand, the highest deities and with the dif-ferent aspects of Time — the great defining factor of all life — and, on the other, with the people may suggest that the people as a whole are regarded by the Javanese as sacred and therefore to be taken seriously into account. This conclusion is strengthened by the fact that some *lakons* tell of the serious consequences which resulted from the unreasonable treatment of these servants by their masters; the *panakawans* go away seeking justice (*lakons* Dewa Lelana[22] and Pandu Bregola[23]), and immediately calamities descend upon the state — a plague spreads through the land and an invasion of a foreign foe is at hand — well-known ominous signs that the balance in the universe is in jeopardy. Only after the masters acknowledge their mistakes is the enemy driven away (normally by the *panakawans* themselves in a disguise provided by the gods) and peace and order is restored to the realm. The power of the people is also symbolized in the *lakon Petruk dadi Ratu*[24] (Petruk becomes a King) wherein, again after a controversy with his master, Petruk becomes — in disguise — a powerful king, defying the strength and skill of his erstwhile masters; at last he is brought into submission but only by his brother and fellow-*panakawan* Gareng. One has also to consider that none of these *lakons* is among the "basic-stories" (*lakon djedjer* or *lakon baku*) which originate from the Indian epics, *Ramayana* and *Mahabharata*; they are all so-called "branch-stories" (*lakon tjarangan*) created by the Javanese themselves and thus clearly revealing Javanese ideals of the ruler-people relationship. Indeed, these *lakons* emphasize the potential power of those who are apparently lowly and insignificant; the moral of these stories seems to be *adja sok njepelekaké*, a common adage which warns men never to look down on what seems insignificant.

---

21 J. J. de Hollander (ed.), "Serat Manik Maja," *VBG*, vol. XXIV, 1852, p. 5.
22 *Serat Padalangan Ringgit Purwa*, Batavia, 1932, Vol. XXII.
23 *Ibid.*, Vol. XV.
24 *Ibid.*, Vol. XXII.

Considering the important role of the *wajang* in Javanese society (not least as a forum for criticism and com-ment on current institutions and affairs) one almost certainly will assume from the above interpretation of the *panakawan*-master relationship that the Javanese see the king and the people as of equal importance, different in terms of function rather than of value.

Nevertheless, another word denoting this relationship does give to the relationship a more complicated pattern. This is the word *momongan*, used repeatedly in different royal edicts, among others in article 7 of the law Angger Ageng of the sixteenth of October 1817,[25] a penal code which obviously had been codified for the specific purpose of regulating the constant disputes between the subjects of Jogjakarta and Surakarta after Mataram's division into the two small kingdoms in 1755. According to Rouffaer,the first dictum was put down in 1771.[26] The question is now whether there are older editions of this statute, in order to justify the use of this word *momongan* as a valid illustration for the whole Later Mataram period. Legal rules and regulations may be drawn for a certain purpose at a certain time, but the underlying legal concepts are normally much older. *Momongan* certainly refers to a legal concept as — in the penal code mentioned earlier — it denotes the subjects under the jurisdiction of a certain administrator, thus indicating a certain attitude from the administrator's point of view. *Momongan* has as its stem the word *momong*, which means to take of with love, to lead;[27] an attitude of constant vigilance and subtle persuasion is implied as well. Generally it is used by the Javanese to describe careful guidance by a trusted servant of his master's children or by parents of their children or again by the husband of his spouse. It expresses a certain duty and a responsibility which places a greater burden on the guardian (*pamong*) than on the guarded, a responsibility which need not stop when the children have reached adulthood. The use of *momongan* as a legal designation for the ruled, therefore, indicates how close the relationship between ruler and ruled should be, and also stresses the role of the ruler in a definitely higher position than the subject, who is

---

25 G. J. Oudemans, *Javaansche Wetten*, Jogjakarta, 1897, Vol. II (Javanese texts), p. 75.

26 G. P. Rouffaer, "Vorstenlanden," in *Adatrechtbundel*, XXXIV, serie D, No. 81, p. 107.

27 Th. Pigeaud, *Javaans-Nederlandsch Handwoordenboek*, Batavia, 1938; and *Java in the 14th Century*, The Hague, 1962, Vol. V. The Old-Javanese *wwang* and *mong* also mean to take care of.

bound into submission by an everlasting feeling of gratitude. The subject's subservience is further strengthened by his belief in the working of fate which has assigned him his proper place in the social hierarchy.

A summary of Javanese thought on the relationship of the king to his subjects will reveal three major concepts:

1. A close, personal relationship accompanied by feelings of mutual love and respect is perceived as the standard mode of social communication.
2. Fate determines man's place in society, whether he will be born a servant or a master. A consequence is that man has no choice but to do his duty as is ordained by fate. These two factors result in a practice of government in which:
3. the ruler (and his officials), in terms of practical administrative policy, must care for his subjects as a parent cares for his children; thus the ruler assumes in fact an attitude of protective superiority, the ruled an attitude of acquiescent subservience.

The King's Position in the Life of the State

Kingship and Islam

In the Javanese concept of the state-organism, the king (*radja, ratu*) is *the* exponent of the micro-cosmos, the state. That the idea of a cosmos divided into a micro-cosmos — the world of man — and a macro-cosmos — the supra-human world — is central to the Javanese world-view is a fact so well-known as to demand no further proof.[28] Inherent in this idea are two factors important to the Javanese understanding of state life: first, there is a parallelism between macro- and micro-cosmos, and, second, there is a necessary interaction between macro- and microcosmos. These two factors determine that social order should be seen as a precise and rigid regulation patterned after the perpetual and exact seasonal changes in nature and the coming and going of stellar constellations. Such a concept

---

28 See further, R. Heine-Geldern, "Conceptions of State and Kingship in Southeast Asia," *The Far Eastern Quarterly*, Vol. 2, November 194 2, pp. 15-30.

of order naturally led to attitudes of traditionalism and conservatism.

The endeavor to create a correspondence between the Great Order and that on earth can be detected in the organizational grouping of the villages (*desa*) into *mantjapat* and *mantjalima*,or the four- and five-group. Although now greatly changed in meaning,[29] originally these names seem to have denoted a four-square arrangement of a village at each cardinal point with one *desa* at the center. The idea of the *mantjanegara*, the outer regions, as distinct from the *nagaragung*, the "Great-", or core-region of the King's realms, is also related to a vision of the macro-cosmos. Although the word *mantja* in modern Javanese is usually understood as "outlying." and thus as "foreign," it is certain that it was derived from the Sanskrit word *pantja*, which means "five," putting us in mind of the five-sectional village alliance mentioned above.[30] The grouping of the king's officials into *keparak kiwa* and *keparak tengen*, or *gedong kiwa* and *gedong tengen*, meaning officials of the left and of the right group, might also be regarded as reflecting conformity with nature's symmetry. While citing de Jonge, Rouffaer noted the preference in Sultan Agung's court in 162 3 for the number four, apparent in the existence of four highest dignitaries, but then again divided two and two into left and right. The four main and the four lesser cardinal points plus the center constitute the number nine, which therefore was also considered holy. Thus, during the Kartasura-period of Later Mataram (approximately 1700), the "Outer" Grand-vizier (Patih Djaba) had eight "outer" subordinate *bupatis* (*bupati djaba*).[31] And Rouffaer was quite right in pointing out the significance of the fact that there were nine *walis*, the traditional sages who proselytized Islam in Java, In the Babad Tjirebon they were further grouped into the four who were born in Java, the four who came from over the sea, and the central one, Sunan Gunung Djati, to complete the number nine.[32] These preferences for certain numbers and arrangements show the age-long persistence of concepts, passing without hindrance through different culture-periods.

A comparison between the period of Hindu-Java and that of Later Mataram brings to light the concept of the king as center of the state

---

29 See further, Chapter III, pp. 101-102.
30 J. Gonda, *Sanskrit in Indonesia*, Nagpur, 1952, p. 91.
31 Rouffaer, *op. cit.*, pp. 56, 57.
32 D. A. Rinkes, "Babad Tjirebon," *VBG*, Vol. LIX, 1911, p. 13.

microcosmos and the pinnacle of the state's status-hierarchy. Since the microcosmos is parallel to the macrocosmos, the Hindu-Javanese king was identified with a god, generally Wisnu, and his queen was identified with the god's *çakti*. The question of a connection between the Hindu Javanese concept of the King and Later Mataram ideas about the role of the King is clarified by Stutterheim's theory about the internment-statues of Old-Javanese kings and queens of East Java.[33] The king-God identification itself had lost its currency in Islamic Java. Indeed Islamic teaching discouraged such an open identification of man with God, a view which caused Seh Wali Lanang, better known under his title Seh Siti Djenar, to be sentenced to death, for he, according to the story, made the fatal mistake of disclosing this secret mystic concept in his preachings.[34] Islamic theology placed the King in a less august position than before, namely as that of the *kalipatullah*, God's representative on earth. Java's rulers assumed this title at a relatively late date;[35] Amangkurat IV (1719-1724) was the first to use it in the form "Prabu Mangku-Rat Senapati Ingalaga Ngabdu'-Rahman Sayidin Panatagama Kalipatullah."[36] In itself it is interesting that this title, which was so serviceable as the Islamic contribution towards enhancing the king's greatness — and not in the least because of its foreign origin — should have been introduced so late. Perhaps this was because the assumption of this title requires the recognition and acceptance of the whole Moslem World; thus the envoys sent by Javanese rulers to Mecca had been able to secure for their masters only the title of "sultan." Only the rulers of Jogjakarta, from 1755 onwards, have consistently used the title of *kalipatullah*,[37] apparently without bothering about the necessary consensus of all the world's Moslems. Furthermore, this difference of title between the rulers of Surakarta and

---

33 W. F. Stutterheim, "The Meaning of the Hindu-Javanese Candi," *Journal of the American Oriental Society*, Vol. 51, No. 1, 1931, pp. 1-15. The popular idea of the king as Wisnu's incarnation is also illustrated in the well-known Ken Angrok legend.

34 Zoetmulder, *op. cit.*, p. 415,

35 What the name "kalifagypan," cited by de Graaf, means is obscure, but it was not the title of Sultan Agung. (H. J. de Graaf, "De Regering van Sultan Agung, Vorst van Mataram," *Verh. KI*, Vol. XXIII, 1958.
p. 103. Also, J. K. J. de Jonge, *De Opkomst van het Nederlandsch Gezag in Oost Indië (1595-1610)*, 's-Gravenhage, 1869, Vol. IV, p. 58.)

36 C. Lekkerkerker, *Land en Volk van Java*, Groningen, 1938, p. 339. *Babad Tanah Djawi* (p. 335) does not mention this title.

37 Lekkerkerker, *op. cit.*, p. 340.

Jogjakarta was obviously more the outcome of stressing the partition of 1755 than that of an active and purposeful policy to assert the king's authority over the entire Moslem world. Another difference in title is that the Sura-karta kings are called *Susuhunan*, those of Jogjakarta, Sultan, also without any further political implications.

Islam's abrogation of the king-god identification did not, however, undermine its essential assertion, the all-dominating and absolute power of the king over his subjects. With the coming of Islam as a new religion, the king and his regional officers had to reassert themselves in the new power-hierarchy in competition with the bearers of Islam, who, in the course of their religious activities, had acquired political influence as well. This power struggle which on and off lasted far into the Later Mataram period usually was decided in favor of the secular authorities. But there always lingered the possibility of a controversy between the representatives of secular power, the *prijaji*, and that of religious leaders, the *kyai*, in establishing social leadership in the Javanese community, and it is noteworthy that in rebellious disturbances up to the present time the *kyai*-element[38] has always been strongly represented.

According to tradition as recorded in the *Babad* literature, at the fall of the Madjapahit monarchy in the first half of the sixteenth century an important place was accorded in religious as well as in political life to the Nine *Walis* (*Wali sanga*), described in Lekkerkerker's study of Java's land and people.[39] Both the *Babad Tanah Djawi* and the *Babad Mataram*, the former written most probably during Sultan Agung's reign (1613-1645)[40] and the latter definitely during the rule of Hamengku Buwana V of Jogjakarta (1822-1826, 1828-1855), relate the important part that the *walis* played in the fall of Madjapahit.[41] The *Babad Mataram* tells the story that before Raden Patah of Demak launched the attack on Madjapahit, "*bubuka saking agama*" (the cause of which was religion), he went first to the venerated Sunan Ngampel, who lived at Ngampel, Surabaja, to ask for his advice and blessing for this important endeavor. Sunan Ngampel told

---

38 *Kyai*: 1. title of veneration for old people in general; 2. title given by the community to a person well-versed in religious questions and the secret doctrines.
39 Lekkerkerker, *op. cit.*, p. 313.
40 H. J. de Graaf, *Over het ontstaan van de Javaanse Rijkskroniek*, Leiden, 1953.
41 *Babad Tanah Djawi*, pp. 28, 29.

him that the time had not yet come because the *"buda"*-king (the Madja-pahit-king professed the Hindu-religion of course) had to reign for one more year. Meanwhile Raden Patah was advised to pray for God's consent, and to ask the blessings of all the *walis*, especially Sunan Kalidjaga and of his stepfather, the Sultan of Palembang.[42] Influence of the *walis* seems to have been so strong that their consent was considered essential before a pretender might ascend the throne. Thus, Sultan Adiwidjaja of Padjang and later Panembahan Senapati[43] indirectly received Sunan Kalidjaga's "testimony" before they ascended the throne. The *Babad Tanah Djawi* narrates Sultan Adiwidjaja's acknowledgment as follows:

> One day *Sunan* Prapen [the then reigning Sunan of Giri] came out in audience. The Sultan of Padjang and the *adipatis* [regional authorities] were sitting in a row. Their retainers sat behind their respective lords. Sultan Padjang was then asked to take a seat close to the *pandita* [Sunan Prapen] who asked [the gathering] for their consensus on his becoming sultan, with the title *Sultan Prabu* Adiwidjaja; [he informed them] that the pandita himself had already given his consent. The time was 1503 [according to the Javanese Era — 1581 A.D.].[44]

Sunan Ngampel's son, the *wali* residing at the important Islamic center of Giri near Gresik, and his successors seem to have played important roles in easing tensions between Mataram's rulers and their mighty vassals of the East-Java coastal regions, led by the *adipati* of Surabaja.[45] Such a mediating function had also been performed by Sunan Kalidjaga and Sunan Kudus of North Central Java, the latter of whom had even allowed himself to get involved in the intrigues of the Demak court when he actively supported the Arja of Djipang's claim to the throne, even going so far as devising a plot to assassinate the succeeding monarch, Sultan Adi-widjaja of Padjang.[46]

---

42 *Babad Mataram* (MS in possession of the Kraton of Jogjakarta, Indonesia), Microfilm, Wason Collection, Cornell University Library, Ithaca, N.Y., p. 82.

43 *Babad Tanah Djawi*, p. 62.

44 *Ibid.*, p. 68.

45 *Ibid.*, p. 99.

46 *Ibid.*, p. 48.

It is remarkable that all these stories can be placed between the fall of Madjapahit and the coming to the throne of Sultan Agung of Mataram, approximately covering the sixteenth century. Thereafter the power of such Moslem sages on the political stage dwindled before the secular might of the king. However, it took Mataram two campaigns to subjugate the priestly stronghold of Giri, whose fame as a center of Moslem learning had spread as far as Ternate in the Moluccas and remained so as late as the end of the seventeenth century.[47] Although in 1635 Sultan Agung had been able, with the help of Surabaja, to take Giri after heavy fighting, in 1680 a second effort had to be made to bring Giri to its knees, now by his grandson, Amangkurat II (1677-1703). This was achieved only after the Mataram and Surabaja troops overran the besieged troops who, with all Giri's material as well as magic powers, made a last grand stand. Another center of Moslem power, Tjirebon, became the formal seat of a branch of the descendants of the *wali* Sunan Gunung Djati, or under another name, Faletehan. It came peacefully under the political supremacy of Mataram by means of a treaty in 1590. This tie was strengthened later when Sultan Agung married a princess of Tjirebon. Sultan Agung called the Sultan of Tjirebon his *guru* (teacher),indicating the semi-ecclesiastical position of the otherwise worldly rulers of Tjirebon. Another center of Islam whose name was respected at the Mataram court was (K)adilangu in the Demak region, where Sunan Kalidjaga had lived in the later part of his life and where his descendants' exceptional position was recognized first by Mataram and later also by the V.O.C. (Dutch East-India Company). The *Babad Tanah Djawi* mentions the presence of Panembahan Widjil of Adilangu at the installation of Pangeran Puger as Paku Buwana I at Semarang in 1703.[48] The Panembahan's presence made legitimate Pangeran Puger's challenge to the rights of Sunan Amangkurat Mas (1703-1708) who, although rightly on the throne, had alienated himself from most of his trusted *adipatis*. Nevertheless, the importance of the lords of Adilangu seems to have been of nominal character only and whatever influence they had was waning steadily; this was reflected in the titles they held during the course of time. The title of Susuhunan Kalidjaga

---

47 H. J. de Graaf, *Geschiedenis van Indonesië*, p. 81.
48 *Babad Tanah Djawi*, p. 277.

was used by the first five descendants. Later, the title was changed into Panembahan Notto-Prodjo (Panembahan Natapradja) by the Surakartan kings. The V.O.C. recognized them as "Pangeran Widjil," while in 1816 the Netherland Indies Government gave them the title Pangerang van Kadilangu or the Pangeran of Adilangu.[49] This decline of titles[50] clearly shows the decline of their importance, which in reality had been more the result of the holiness emanating from Sunan Kalidjaga's tomb than that of the religious activities of the descendants. Paku Buwana I refers to the tomb's holiness when reminiscing about the *pusakas* (holy inherited objects) of the *kraton*:

> I am very much depressed that all the *pusakas* have been taken by my son the king [Amangkurat Mas], but I know that, even if all the other *pusakas* should be taken away, if only the Demak-mosque and the tomb of Adilangu remain, this will suffice. Only these two are the true *pusakas* of Java.[51]

In examining the important Moslem centers of power we cannot overlook the role of the panembahans of Kadjoran, a locality in the Klaten area of Surakarta, whose lords were related to the founder of the Tembajat-sanctuary, the *wali* Sunan Bajat.[52] These lords of Kadjoran had repeatedly been a great nuisance to Mataram because of their reluctant attitude toward their overlord. Although bound by ties of marriage to the Mataram dynasty,[53] they were not reluctant to take up a rebellious cause, in which Trunadjaja, son-in-law of Raden Kadjoran or Panembahan Rama,had played the principal role. An open breach in 1677 between Mataram and Kadjoran led finally to the extermination of the latter (1679). To this

---

49 *Selection of important documents belonging to the Collection Kern and Gobee* (in the possession of the Koninklijk Instituut voor Taal-, Land- en Volkenkunde, The Hague), Microfilm, Wason Collection, Cornell University Library, Ithaca, N.Y., Film I, no. 24.

50 According to the *Babad Mataram*, the next five successors of Sunan Kalidjaga were: Sunan Adi, Panembahan Pangulu, Panembahan Ketib, Panembahan Agung, Panembahan Sabrang, followed by a succession of Pangerans with the same name Widjil. Thus, only two bore the title "sunan." *Babad Mataram*, p. 10.

51 *Babad Tanah Djawi*, p. 301.

52 The fact that at one time the great Sultan Agung had gone to the extent of building a gate and a *pendapa* at the site of the holy graves of Tembajat (1633) confirms its importance.

53 H. J. de Graaf, "Het Kadjoran Vraagstuk," *Djawa*, Vol. 20 (1940), nos. 4-5, pp. 274, 276.

uprising Professor de Graaf has given his attention in an article of some length.[54]

With the elimination of these centers of religious power one can say that secular Mataram's dominance had become a fact. But the controversy between religion and the state has never been permanently settled and, in Java, religious motives have frequently been used to justify political opposition. This was so in the Java War of 1825-30, for instance, when the distinctly religious title *Ngabdulkamid Eroetjakra Sajidin Panatagama Chalifat Rasulu'llah Sain* was taken by Pangeran Dipanegara. The important position of Kyai Madja, the prince's spiritual tutor, and the distinctly Arabic, thus Moslem, garb[55] worn by the prince (the *djubah* or robe and the *serban* or turban) also emphasized the religious banner under which the war was fought.

It is therefore easy to understand that the rulers of Later Mataram very early tried to recapture undivided sacro-political power,[56] which, in the period of transition to Islam, was slipping out of their hands. These efforts to restore the unity of authority can be detected in the rank-denoting titles which the first rulers of Mataram had assumed. As indicated in Pigeaud's study, *Java in the 14th Century*, the usual title of local lords and chiefs of some prominence was *adipati* (chief, governor). *Bhupati*, during the latter half of the Later Mataram period, came to be the functional title of the higher group of dignitaries in the king's administration. *Pati*, translated by "ruler," could denote the king himself as well as other dignitaries.[57] In Javanese literature we can find these words in shorter form: *dipati*[58] or *pati*, titles under which Dipati Ukur and Pati (J)unus appear. Citing Pigeaud, *Senapati* is "a title name of prominent chieftains of rural estates given by the 15th and 16th Century kings of Demak and Pajang" to, among others, the lord of Pasir in the western Banjumas area and also to the chief of Mataram.[59] But in the quest for the highest place in the social hierarchy of

---

54 *Ibid.*

55 H. J. de Graaf, *Geschiedenis van Indonesië.* See the picture opposite p. 304.

56 According to Islamic theology, temporal and spiritual authority is never divided. There is only the overall authority of the Shari'a, the prophetically revealed law of Islam. See E. I. J. Rosenthal, *Political Thought in Medieval Islam*, Cambridge, 1962, pp. 22, 23.

57 Pigeaud, *Java in the 14th Century*, Vol. V, Glossary and Index.

58 J. Gonda, *Sanskrit in Indonesia*, p. 34.

59 Pigeaud, *Java in the 14th Century*, Vol. IV, p. 375.

homage and reverence, the secular rulers did not seem content with these titles or even the title sultan, with its aura of foreign superiority, for which Sultan Agung had exerted considerable effort (1641). On the other hand, the popularity of the great Moslem *Walis* had become a political factor with which they had to deal seriously. In 1624 Sultan Agung therefore took the title of "Susuhunan Ngalaga Mataram"; this new title, *sunan*, had been a title of the *Walis* or their successors and this only for Giri for three generations and apparently for Kadilangu for five generations. The word itself is of Javanese origin and simply means "he who is honored" and comes from the stem *suwun* (to bear on one's head), similar to the also frequently used title *panembahan* which is derived from *sembah*, the act of doing reverence by lifting joined hands to one's nose or forehead. Nevertheless the title of *susuhunan*, its honorific character heightened above that of the simpler *sunan* by reduplication of the first syllable *su-* and by interpolation of the syllable *-hu-*, had become so much more magnificent than the title of sultan that Amangkurat I, the immediate successor of Sultan Agung, no longer used the latter title. *Susuhunan* and its variant *sinuwun* have been used consistently ever since. With the assumption of this important — from the point of view of cosmological absoluteness — title, sacral and temporal power was gathered into one hand never to be released again, and the clergy returned to being only a part of the king's administration. The importance of the title *susuhunan* is expressed by de Graaf in the following words:

This [title] *susuhunan* unmistakably conveyed that its bearer, decorated with the highest imaginable sacred title, must himself be God's envoy also, and moreover a daily present one. His descendants, — and this would be proven by custom — would also be called *susuhunan* and their [beneficent] influence would spread over the realm. With this, the divinity of the Hindu-Javanese kings was revived, although under a new name and in a different form. Even the sacrosanct tomb of the king, the *tjandi*, received a successor in the holy *pasarejan* [grave] on top of the Ima Giri.[60]

---

60 H. J. de Graaf, "Titels en Namen van Javaanse Vorsten en Groten uit de 16e en de 17e Eeuw," *Bijdragen*, Vol. 109, 1953, p. 77.

The King's Task

It is obvious that such an accumulation of powers in one hand for political reasons would nourish the ideology of monarchical absolutism.

The Javanese believed that the king was the one and only medium linking the micro-cosmos of man with the macro-cosmos of the gods. This was expressed in Pangeran Puger's words when Pangeran Tjakraningrat urged him to rise against his nephew, the arrogant Amangkurat III (1703-1708) :

> ...if a man should dare to rise against his king, misfortune will overcome him, because the king is Allah's *warana*.[61]

In literary language, *warana* means "deputy" or "representative," but its literal meaning is "screen"; thus, in this context, the king is the screen through which man must pass to reach God and, conversely, through which God must pass to reach man. Since the king was seen as the sole intermediary between man and God, it was not strange that his decisions were thought to be unchallengeable and his powers without limitation; his decisions were God's will and his actions were God's management.

The idea of absolute and supreme power is expressed in the phrase *wenang murba wisesa* which was applied both to God's omnipotence and to the king's power,[62] thus again showing that the king's position was seen as a reflection of that of God. God is titled *Sang Murba-wisesa*, the Supreme Ruler. The use of the words *purba* (rule) and *wisesa* (highest authority) is not restricted to modern Javanese alone; it is found in older texts with the same meaning. For instance, in the *Nawaruci* of 1615 A.D., *wenang wisesa ing sanagari*[63] expresses the king's supreme authority in his whole realm and, in the *Kidung Pamancangah, sang amurwa bhumi* is the title of the king. Thus the king is placed at the pinnacle of the social order, far beyond the reach of the common people. This point of view at one time gave rise to the idea of the king as a politically inactive power, the *ratu pinandita* (the sage king), from whom emanated beneficent influences,

---

61 *Babad Tanah Djawi*, p. 266.
62 Zoetmulder, *op. cit.*, p. 343; and Gonda, *op. cit.*, pp. 305, 424.
63 Cited in Gonda, *op. cit.* , pp. 203, 318.

permeating his whole realm. Active participation in the affairs of the state was left to his dignitaries, especially the *patih* (the grand vizier) whose usually non-royal descent conformed with his special technical task. In the *wajang* literature such an attitude towards the king is illustrated in the figure of King Judistira, the eldest of the Pandawas, who had "white blood," never gave vent to anger and dressed very simply.[64] He was so truthful — except once during the Bratajuda (the war between Pandawa and Korawa) — that the gods made him the only human being whose feet never touched the earth. In a work of 1883 by the monarch Paku Buwana IX (1861-1893) entitled *Wulang Radjaputra*,the idea of the king's beneficence radiating over the kingdom comes to the fore.

> God's rahmat (mercy) is in [the king's] heart, from whence it overflows, covering the whole country, which, if in ardent love]of God], will be under the protecting shade of the king. The common people, humble, all want to work their fields in order to prevent shortage of food; thus is the king's mercy: the welfare of the village lies in the density of its population.[65]

The question of what role the king should play in the organizational structure of the worldly order (the *negara* — the state) will be discussed next. In the *gara-gara* scene of a *wajang* play nature is in a state of upheaval, a sign that a hero is in distress. Here one can see clearly, first, the interaction between the two cosmic orders and, second, the gods' cardinal function of restoring the cosmic order, which in this case has been thrown into a state of imbalance by the acts of man. The main task of a king parallels that of his celestial prototypes; he must maintain or restore order to his world, the state, so that not only in structure but also in function the micro-cosmos would mirror the macro cosmos. The king's powers as restorer of order are thought to be so great that he can even overcome epidemics of truly macro-cosmic magnitude. Processions carrying the sacred *pusaka* Kandjeng Kyai Tunggul Wulung (a holy relic of the kraton of Jogjakarta in the form of a standard) were organized in

---

64 Hardjowirogo, *op. cit.* , pp. 76, 77.
65 Paku Buwana IX, *Serat Wara Isjwara*, ed. Padmasusastra, Surakarta, 1898, p. 36.

Jogjakarta during the plague epidemics of 1932 and 1948.[66] They were an expression of confidence in the king's power to restore order rather than in that of the *pusaka*; indeed, the relic, though certainly powerful, was thought of as a tool in the hands of the lord of the worldly order. Selosoemardjan explains the *pusaka*'s contributory role in these words:

> ...certain *pusakas* in the palace of the Sultan, (spears, Javanese daggers called krises, or flags) have magical powers which support any Sultan who is legally and cosmologically entitled to rule over the country.[67]

For that matter, the names of the kings of Jogjakarta and Surakarta and of several princes of rank usually refer to firmness and stability. For instance, Paku (of Paku Buwana) means "nail" and Hamengku (from Hamengku Buwana) means "to have on one's lap" or to care for.

Two ideas seemed to dominate the Javanese view of order (*tata* or less commonly, *krama*). They are, first, the idea of fixed regularity and, second, the idea of non-interference. This view, of course, was the result of an agrarian nation's special awareness of pattern in nature's behavior. Clinging to the security of the known, the Javanese thought that interfering with the regular, the fixed, might disturb the Order, the results of which — because of the principle of interaction — might be of calamitous proportions. This idea of non-interference will be reflected in state administration too.[68]

The king's primary duties in the political sphere are to guard against disturbances and to restore the order if any such disturbance should occur. This stress on guarding against discrepancies and evil is also expressed in the words *ndjaga tata-tentreming pradja* (guarding the order and tranquillity of the state) which is the main duty of the *pangreh pradja* or body of royal officials for the "outer"-service. During the introductory *kanda* (narrative) to a *wajang* play, the puppeteer (*dalang*) describes the welfare of the country, praising the luxuriance of all things

---

66 See for the *upatjaras* also: J. P. H. Duyvendak, *Inleiding tot de Ethnologie van de Indonesische Archipel*, Groningen, 1954, pp. 136-138.

67 Selosoemardjan, *Social Changes in Jogjakarta*, Ithaca, N.Y., 1962, pp. 17, 18.

68 See Chapter I, p. 2ff. and Chapter III, p. 90.

planted and the inex-pensiveness of all things one buys. He also tells the audience that trade flourishes in the country because there are no "disturbances on the roads," that the cattle and poultry roam through the countryside unattended because of the "nonexistence of evil-doers," and that "marauding enemies" are far away. There are "no disagreements between the king's officials," and therefore the state stands high in the regard of other countries even those on the "outer islands." Thus, the *dalang* describes the order and peace of the state (*tata-tentreming pradja*) in terms of an absence of disturbance. In describing the royal virtues the *dalang* says that the king

> …is generous in giving alms, gives clothes to those who have none, gives a cane to those who slip, shelter to those scorched by the sun, food to those in hunger, consolation to the heavy of heart, a torch to those in darkness; he clears the thicket where it grows dense…[69]

Thus, one can see that the king's intervention is thought necessary only if circumstances are out of balance, abnormal. Originating changes in the "normal" order is regarded as unthinkable, for innovation is fundamentally incompatible with the view that order is an undisturbed system, a pattern fixed by tradition and custom.

Any unavoidable change then must be justified with analogies or other devices which will fit it into the fixed pattern of unchanging regularity. The semblance of continuity is in this way preserved and explained.[70] The well-known story of the,death of the virtuous king Puntadewa (Judistira) of Ngamarta may be taken as a clear example of such justification by analogy — here by similarity of sounds. One day, the most important *wali*, Sunan Kalidjaga, met a very ancient man who claimed to be King Puntadewa. The latter, already many centuries old, explained to the *wali* that he could not die because no one could read the *Serat Kalimasada* which he possessed. The old king asked the sage "the way to death." The *wali* then examined the letter and discovered that it was none other than

---

69 Ch. te Mechelen (ed.), "Drie Teksten van Toneelstukken uit de Wajang-Poerwa", *VBG*, Vol. XLIII, 1882, p. 1.
70 About this idea of continuity see also: C. C. Berg, "The Islamization of Java," *Studia Islamica*, IV, 1955, part II.

the *Kalimah Sahadat*, the Islamic confession of faith. Sunan Kalidjaga read it for the eldest of the Pandawa, and Judistira then died in peace, freed from the ties of ignorance.[71] A grave, exceptionally long, behind the holy mosque of Demak, is still popularly thought to be Judistira's final resting place. With this ingenious device, the similarity between the sound of the Sanskrit "kalimasada" and the Arabic "kalimah sahadat," the Javanese thus laid a tie of continuity between two seemingly contrasting, but for them, intrinsically equal historical periods.

The Ideal King

Burdened with the temptations of unlimited power and with the immense and singular responsibility of preserving order in his world, the king had to be of extraordinary excellence and quality. The Javanese assume that such excellence must be evident in the physical countenance of the ruler, and a bad monarch is usually identified as afflicted with a deformity. In the Indian *Mahabharata*, the blind king, Destarata of Ngastina, is always pictured as a just man who opposes the evil intentions of his hundred sons, the *Kaurawas*. In the Javanese *wajang*, however, he is pictured as an unreliable person who does not feel it beneath his dignity to advise his sons to deprive their cousins, the *Pandawas*, of what is rightfully theirs.[72] But because of his deformity he is also cheated several times.[73] Sunan Amangkurat III (1703-1708), also known under his surname Sunan Mas (the Golden Sunan), was nicknamed *pun Kentjet* (the Crippled One) because of his sensual improprieties which earned him the contempt of his time; the *Babad Tanah Djawi*, even though a royal chronicle, does not hesitate to record the words of *tumenggung* Djajengrana of Surabaja who said of the king, at the time in despair, facing the attacks of his usurper uncle, Pangeran Puger:

And then the king, I noticed, had lost his *tjahja* (gleam of the

---

71 Hardjowirogo, *op. cit.* , p. 76. See also: G. W. J. Drewes, *Drie Javaansche Goeroe's*, Leiden, 1925, p. 23. Here this story is connected with a tomb of a Sech Djambu Karang in the district of Tjahjana, regency of Purba-lingga, Central Java.
72 Mechelen, *op. cit.* , pp. 117-120, in the *lakon* "Pandu Papa."
73 *Ibid.*, pp. 95, 96, in the *lakon* "Narasoma."

countenance) ; he looked pale like a Chinaman whose stomach is aching.

At this the audience roared with laughter.[74] To say such a think about a king is something almost unheard of; he must have sunk very low in this official's esteem. Professor Hoesein Djajadiningrat sees these disparaging views of Amang-kurat III as a means of justifying Pangeran Puger's rebellion.[75] The *lambang-pradja* is a symbolic narrative in which each reign is described in poetic terms; the reign of Sunan Mas is characterized as *lung gadung semune rara nglikasi* (the tendril of a *gadung*-plant, also an allusion to a girl twisting yarn), which alludes to the Sunan's intelligence but also to his unseemly character.[76]

How did the Javanese picture his ideal king? The king's power was understood as unlimited. He could not be regulated by worldly means, but within himself there was a force reflecting, or higher still, identical with the Divine Soul (Hyang Suksma Kawekas), which checked his individual will. The Javanese thought of the ideal king as one constantly seeking for this internal divine guidance. In a *wajang-lakon*, the *dalang* never fails to relate in his *kanda* (narrative) that the king retires into the inner chambers of the palace after holding an audience, changes into the plain clothes of a *pandita* (sage) and then enters the *sanggar pamudjan* (chamber of worship) to "acquire knowledge of God's will." And the required presence of three important officials at court, one of which was the astrologer, undoubtedly also served the king's need for divine guidance. Panembahan Senapati was said to have advised Pangeran Benawa (whom he placed on the throne of Padjang to succeed his father — only nominally — as sultan) to appoint these three officials:

...first a *pandita* (sage), second a *tijang petang iladuning palak palakijah* (astrologer), third an *ahli tapa* (ascetic). If you find

---

74 *Babad Tanah Djawi*, p. 273.

75 Hoesein Djajadiningrat, *Critische beschouwingen over de Sadjarah Banten*, Haarlem, 1913, p. 241. It must be said however that Amangkurat Mas was one of the fiercest opponents of Dutch political encroachment in Java.

76 J. A. B. Wiselius, "Djaja Baja," *Bijdragen*, Vol. VII (19), 1872, p. 192ff. These allegories are to be found in the *Serat Djaja Baja* which seems to have been written or re-written after the Java War (1825-1830). See also Padmosoekotjo, *op. cit.*, pp. 52-53.

difficulties in governing your kingdom, ask the *pandita*, if you
want to know about what is yet to come, ask the astrologer, if you
want to know about magic powers, ask the ascetic.[77]

Divine guidance expressed itself in the *kawitjaksanan* of the king, a
rare and highly esteemed capacity, which not only endowed the holder
with the widest possible range of knowledge but also the deepest
awareness of realities and a sense of justice. That there is a wide range
of meaning in the word *witjaksana* is illustrated in the several existing
Javanese dictionaries and word lists where it is explained as "highly
excellent," as "wise, experienced, skillful, intelligent" or "learned," and
again as "with clear insight."[78] For the Indonesian word "*bidjaksana*"
of the same origin, Gonda gives the meaning "practical wisdom or
skill."[79] The Sanskrit original of the word, *wicaksana*, denotes sagacity,
experience or familiarity. A Javanese, Poerwadarminta, attaches two
meanings to this word; first, being "aware, *waskita* (able to see into
things kept secret, like man's thought, etc.)" and, secondly, "able to use
one's *budi* (thinking ability, reason) rightly." *Kawitjaksanan* denoted
the greatest skill not only in weighing subtly the possible advantages
or disadvantages of one's decision but also a keen sense of judgment
in the handling of situations, primarily to preserve the cosmic order.
In practice this amounts to a policy of checking and balancing; that
is, avoiding those disturbing open clashes that were not absolutely
necessary. Significantly, Paku Buwana X (1893-1939) of Surakarta
was called by the Javanese of his own time the *ratu panutup*, "the last
king," for he was the last king who lived according to the tradition of
grandeur and royal serenity. He had acquired the surname "*witjaksana*"
because his reign was marked by tranquillity; it was irrelevant that
this tranquillity was not the result of an active and stimulating policy
towards progress, but of helpless obedience to the wishes of the
Netherlands-Indies government.

---

77 *Babad Tanah Djawi*, p. 96.
78 P. Jansz, *Javaansch-Nederlandsch Woordenboek*, Bandoeng, 1906; T. Roorda, *Javaansch-Nederlandsch Handwoordenboek*, Amsterdam, 1901; G. W. J. Drewes, *Eenvoudig hedendaagsch Javaansch Proza*, Leiden, 1946, Word-list; and J. Gonda, *op. cit.*, p. 305.
79 Gonda, *loc. cit.*

The concept of *kawitjaksanan* was a surprisingly comprehensive tool for statesmanship in traditional Javanese society, but its totally abstract and general character limited its usefulness in facing the realities of government. One might even say that this idea put more emphasis on the king's absolute and lone power of decision over all matters, forcing him to master all possible factors each time he acted. Numerous books on practical politics had to be written instructing the king on problems ranging from how a king should comport himself to how he should choose his officials or on what are the kingly taboos. Most of these works are quite general; hardly any are of a specifically technical character. This could be expected because technical trifles could *not* belong to the kingly sphere. In these writings, true to the spirit of conservatism, stress was put on the exemplary behavior and meritorious acts of figures of the past, in history as well as in legend. And again, as we have seen above, the *wajang* served as a never-failing source. Consequently these stories and histories of famous characters are to be found scattered through all types of literature. At any rate, the Javanese never took up a book without seeking for some instruction in what he read, which, considering the preponderantly sacral character of literature in old Java, is not surprising. Some, however, were specially written for the sole purpose of instruction.[80]

The best-known text on kingly attitude is the part of the *Serat Rama*[81] which records Rama's advice to Wibisana, whom he had placed on the throne of Ngalengka to replace his late brother King Dasamuka (or Rawana in Sanskrit). This part is called the *Asta-brata*, "the Eight Life-rules,"[82] or "the Eight (statesman's) Virtues" according to Pigeaud's dictionary. The *Asta-brata* was so popular that it was taken over in full both in the *Nitisruti*, allegedly written by Pangeran Karanggajam of Padjang in the year 1612, and in the later *Nitipradja* dated 1641.[83] It was also cited in the so-called *Angger Djugulmuda* which was said to be the work of a Sultan

---

80 See Chapter I, p. 12.

81 Kyai Jasadipura I, *Serat Rama*, Semarang, 1919, pp. 432-435. The *Serat Rama* is a translation by the court writer Jasadipura I (1729-1802) of the older Old-Javanese *Ramayana*.

82 The *Serat Rama* used the word *lampah* as a translation, a Krama-word (Ngoko-form: *laku*) which can mean "(ascetic) life-rule." See Appendix III.

83 Poerbatjaraka, *op. cit.*, pp. 102, 103. Professor Poerba-tjaraka thought this dating to be pure nonsense.

of Demak.[84] Apart from being part of a cherished story, the reason for the popularity of the *Asta-brata* might be traced to the fact that the eight virtues prescribed for the king were there identified with those of eight *dewas* (deities) of the Hindu pantheon, which made the sanctity of these virtues unquestionable. These eight deities apparently were those known in Indian mythology as the *Lokapalas* or Guardians of the Universe, four at first for the four cardinal points and later extended to eight to include the intermediate quarters.[85] The *Serat Rama* mentions the same eight deities although not associated with directions. They are respectively Endra, Jama, Surja, Tjandra, Baju, Kuwera, Baruna and Brama. That these eight deities together form the ideal characterization of a king again indicates the king's central place in *his* world order. Not one of the eight characteristics may be missing. This was stressed by Rama:

> beware, the eight deities must be within you ...you may not leave out one of the eight, or your kingship will show a deficiency.[86]

The king, then, should possess these eight virtues:
1. Unlimited *dana*, "beneficence," attributed to *batara* Endra, master of all the lesser gods;
2. Ability to repress all evil, attributed to the deity of death, Jama;
3. Kindly persuasiveness and wise conduct, attributed to the sun-god, Surja;
4. Lovingness, attributed to *batara* Tjandra;
5. Keen awareness and deep insight, attributed to the god of the winds, Baju;
6. Generosity with material wealth and recreation, attributed to the god of worldly fortune, Kuwera;
7. Sharp and ruthless intelligence in facing difficulties of any kind, attributed to the god of the seas, Baruna; and
8. Fiery courage and spirited determination in opposing any enemy, attributed to fire-god Brama.[87]

---

84 Tjabang Bagian Bahasa Jogjakarta, *Ngungak isining Serat Astabrata*, Jogjakarta, 1958, p. 20.
85 A. L. Basham, *The Wonder that was India*, London, 1956, p. 314.
86 Jasadipura I, *op. cit.*, p. 432.
87 For a translation of the *Asta Brata*, see Appendix III.

These characteristics indeed form a very realistic understanding of the problems of state politics, encompassing benevolent love as well as unrelenting harshness and forgetting neither the importance of material wealth nor the power of intelligence. But it also emphasizes the extraordinary and indeed superhuman demands of the kingly ideal, the futility of which the Javanese fully realized. Therefore he was not averse to describing the royal reigns — and so the kings themselves — in the surprisingly well-chosen and frank allusions of the *Serat Djaja Baja*, a secret and sacred document to the Javanese because it reveals the future.[88] To give another example, the reign of Amangkurat I (1648-1677), notably a cruel king, was described as *Kalpa sru semune kenaka putung*, "the harsh time of the broken nails." The harsh period indicates the cruelty of the king's reign, and the broken claws the many commanders whom he put to death unnecessarily. Paku Buwana I (1703-1719), already old when he came to the throne, was pictured as *Gunung kendeng semune kenya musoni*. The *gunung kendeng* (long mountain) refers to his old age, while his habit of meddling with trifles was likened to the cleaning of cotton by a girl, a job so unimportant that it was usually done by children and old people. The *Babad Tanah Djawi* displayed a great deal of frankness too in relating stories about the king and his officials. The excessive cruelties of Amangkurat I seen in the *Babad Tanah Djawi* as a sign of his coming downfall, the apparent weakness of Amangkurat II who relied wholly on his brother Pangeran Pu-ger's abilities, the disgust which a cowardly deed inspired — all this was told in words which left no doubt as to their import.[89]

From the example of gods the Javanese then looked to examples of great men of the past, so again to tradition. In the available *piwulangs*, which all date from the nineteenth century, emphasis is placed on the examples of the *leluhur*, the royal ancestors, notably Panembahan Senapati and Sultan Agung, but also on the (for the Middle-Javanese) most noted of the Nine *Walis*, Sunan Kalidjaga.[90] For the Mangkunegaran principality, its first ruler, the well-known Raden Mas Said, was the main example.[91]

88 See p. 40.
89 *Babad Tanah Djawi*, pp. 154, 237, 231.
90 Paku Buwana IV, *Wulangreh*, p. 37; also Paku Buwana IX, *op. cit.*, in the "Wulang Putra."
91 Mangkunegara IV, *Dwidja Isjwara*, ed. Padmasusastra, Surakarta, 1899, p. 43.

Of course figures from the *wajang* and other persons, even some not of royal descent, were taken in the *piwulangs* as "historic" figures worthy of emulation. In all of these personages the characteristic most praised was their spiritual strength in severely restricting their worldly pleasures. Such *laku* (conduct, behavior) demonstrated their sincere and consistent determination (*tekad*)[92] to attain a certain goal, the most laudable of which was acquiring *ngelmu* or *ngelmu kasampurnan* (spiritual knowledge). Sunan Kalidjaga, for instance, is said to have done *tapa* (ascetic meditation) for years with such a profound firmness that the roots of trees grew over him and Sunan Bonang, who had commanded him to do *tapa* to test him, had difficulty in finding him again.[93] Panembahan Senapati did his *tapa* in a river, allowing himself to be carried off by the current.[94] In the same way Sultan Agung earned the power to transport himself every Friday to the holy city of Mecca itself, returning immediately after saying his prayers to his *kraton* in Kuta Gede, "in the wink of an eye." But apart from acquiring supernatural power or knowledge (*sekti*), the performance of *tapa* had its greatest value in the advantage it gave to one's descendants and, for a king, to his people and his entire kingdom. Mangkune-gara IV attributed the prosperity of his princedom to the difficulties — also considered as a form of ascetic practice — which the founder of the Mangkunegaran House endured and his perseverance in the face of all kinds of discomfort in his fight for an independent realm.[95] Paku Buwana IX cites an even clearer example: the *demang* (an official directly above the village-headman) Singaparna renounced his conjugal rights in order to become an ascetic, and so, through the female line, he had as a descendant a king, Paku Buwana VIII (1858-1861).[96] From these examples one can deduce how very important the *laku* was for the ruling Javanese elite, and this was logical for only self control could prevent misuse of power by an absolute king. The king had to possess a personality of not merely flawless but of incorruptible righteousness which, according to the Javanese, could be achieved only through this method.

---

92 Ki Hadjar Dewantara, *Beoefening van Letteren en Kunst in het Pakoe Alamsche geslacht*, Jogjakarta, 1931, p. 26, "Serat Piwoelang," couplets 2, 3.

93 *Babad Mataram*, p. 30.

94 *Babad Tanah Djawi*, pp. 77, 78.

95 Mangkunegara IV, *op. cit.*, p. 44, in the "Pariwijata."

96 Paku Buwana IX, *op. cit.*, p. 77, in the part "Wulang Putra."

Following the examples of great ancestors and predecessors also led to the rigid observance of *wewalers* (taboos) imposed by the ancestors and usually based on personal experience. These taboos ranged from the observance of *dina sangars* (calamitous days) to the use of certain kinds of wood for the shaft of a lance or the obedience to certain customs in certain localities. Paku Buwana IV in his *Wulangreh* meticulously enumerated these *wewalers*.[97]

It is perhaps interesting to examine further the period covering the end of the eighteenth century and through the nineteenth century. Much of the writing of this period reveals Javanese ideals as well as realities. This period seems to have had an intensive court-culture[98] which resulted in a profusion of literary achievement. For example, most of the works of the Later Mataram period listed in Poerbatja-raka's book on Javanese literature were written during this particular period.[99] And indeed there are no *piwulangs* from any other period, which of course does not mean that they did not exist previously. *Piwulangs* were meant to fulfill specific contemporary needs, although of course they were based on traditional views and ideas.[100] A careful reading of this genre of literature discloses the period's atmosphere of regret, of uncertainty and helplessness in the face of a reality too often unrelated to accepted standards of conduct.

In the *Serat Djaja Baja*, the time of the Java War was interpreted as *Praptane kalabendu ing Semarang lan Tembajat*, "the coming of *Kala* and Anger (of God) to Semarang and Tembajat." Such a characterization implies the deterioration of the people's welfare and the ineptitude of its government. Semarang referred to the Dutch and Tembajat to the Javanese. The book further comments: "The movements of the people are without purpose. They go from the North to the South and back again; finally they die without having gone in pilgrimage."[101] The last king cited in the *Serat Djaja Baja* was Paku Buwana IV (1788-1820),so this period immediately preceding the Java War was considered a time of decline, a

---

97 Paku Buwana IV, *op. cit.*, pp. 37, 38.
98 D. H. Burger, *Structural Changes in Javanese Society*, trans. Leslie H. Palmier, Translation Series, Modern Indonesia Project, Cornell University, Ithaca, N.Y., 1956, pp. 11-14.
99 Poerbatjaraka, *op. cit.*, p. 170ff.
100 See for comparison Ki Hadjar Dewantara, *op. cit.* This pamphlet describes the literary activities of the Paku Alam House of Jogjakarta. For examples of *piwulang*, see pp. 26, 32, 35.
101 Wiselius, *op. cit.* , p. 186.

time in which society lay in a state of abject inertia. Should we not see the Java War, then, in its five-year long severity as a desperate effort to recapture past grandeur and independence of kingship? Paku Buwana IX (1861-1893) wrote of a *bupati* who could be corrupted by bribes and that one could buy a *mantri*-rank (lower official) and think nothing of the impertinence.[102] Veth, perhaps with a shudder of disgust, wrote about "the population of the *Kraton*":

> Among the populace as well as among the dignitaries there must be a terrible perversity of morals; disgusting stories went around about it.[103]

Although undoubtedly very much exaggerated, these words, written in the 1880's, pictured the mood of the time. Louw's monumental work on the Java War also described corrupt practices in Javanese society, especially the heavy burden of taxes laid on the population.[104] Dr. Johns mentions "the present day assessment of [the Sufi orders] as other-worldly and escapist institutions, representing Islam in decline,"[105]
This assessment is applicable to the period we are discussing for Islam in general, for in religious life, too, standards were deteriorating. Paku Buwana IX made this clear by his words,

> *pengulus* (ecclesiastical dignitaries) forget to pray, constantly having their cockerels fought in the ring.[106]

And it is possible that the *wajang lakons* which depict the power of the people[107] were composed during this period as a warning to those concerned not to oppress the common people. The *lakon Petruk dadi Ratu* (Petruk becomes a king) portrays Petruk, the clown, as king of

102 Paku Buwana IX, *op. cit.* , p. 185.

103 P. J. Veth, *Java*, Haarlem, 1875, Vol. III, p. 676.

104 P. J. F. Louw, *De Java Oorlog*, Batavia, 1894, p. 12, citing the "Verslag van den Assistent Resident van Jogjakarta," dated June 13, 1824.

105 A. H. Johns, "Sufism as a Category in Indonesian Literature and History," *Journal of Southeast Asian History*, Vol. II, July, 1961, p. 21.

106 Paku Buwana IX, *op. cit.*, p. 185.

107 Chapter II, p. 24.

"Burneo,"[108] obviously meaning the island of Kalimantan (Borneo). Therefore the *lakon* could not be very old as the name does not appear in the older literature, where Kalimantan, or at least part of it, was known as Sukadana.[109]

In the *piwulangs* of Paku Buwana IX and Mangkunegara IV as well as in the *Wulangreh* of Paku Buwana IV (1788-1820) there are repeated complaints about the unseemly behavior of a younger generation filled with pride, lacking deep knowledge, and using position for personal enrichment.[110] This indicates that the younger generation, forced to comply with the new standards of time, had begun to desert established values.

The writings of the kings cited above give the impression that the monarchs themselves did not feel that they had enough power to deal firmly with all these anomalies. They tried to compensate by giving examples of good and evil and stressing the virtues of a life of righteousness and abstinence. Such helplessness is largely explained by the humiliation inflicted on them by the Netherlands-Indies Government which had reduced their power and, not least, their very basis of wealth — population and farmland — to a mere fraction of what it had been.[111] But it is also true that the Javanese themselves can be blamed. Instead of seeking new and more effective means to face the new situation, the monarchs fell back on the traditional "proven" methods, which they sought to apply while lacking their previous power. Javanese society in general seemed to be afflicted with a loss of vitality, looking backwards towards great figures of the past but lacking the determination to surpass or even equal what had been achieved. The self-assurance of a Ki Adipati Martalaja, who grasped a Dutch envoy by his neck to force him down into the *sila*-posture (sitting

---

108 *Serat Padalangan Ringgit Purwa*, Vol. XXII, p. 20. The name "Borneo" certainly was not created by the Javanese but probably, at least in its misspelling, originated with the Europeans. It must have struck an odd note in the Javanese ear because of its unfamiliar sound and therefore was appropriate for the kingdom of the clownish second son of Semar.

109 De Graaf, *Geschiedenis van Indonesië*, p. 107. Mechelen, *op. cit.*, p. 30. See also Pigeaud, *Java in the 14th Century*, Vol. III, p. 16, where, in the summation of territories under Madjapahit, Kalimantan was not named as an entity although many of the regional names undoubtedly referred to places on the island.

110 Paku Buwono IV, *op. cit.*, pp. 4, 31.

111 See also P. J. Veth, *op. cit.*, Vol. III, pp. 567-568, for the extensive intervention of the Dutch in the affairs of the two Javanese kingdoms. See further Chapter III, p. 118.

crosslegged) before Amangkurat II (1677-1703) at Tegal,[112] or the tone of respect with which another envoy described the fierce countenance of Sultan Agung,[113] could scarcely be found in writings of these periods of stagnation. In this atmosphere of impotence there were even warnings against reaching too high to the examples of the great such as Sultan Agung or Sunan Kalidjaga, because the former was a "king-sage"; it sufficed to ask his benevolent influence and to take a lesson from the latter's youthful life of abandon, which, however, was precisely what the young men of Paku Buwana IX's time were not doing.[114] These tendencies towards decline might account for Mangkunegara IV's attempt to revive the spirit of *satrija*-ship (knighthood) with the — again traditional — idea of *kawirjan*, the virtues of bravery and noble conduct.[115]

It is strange that this period of political decline should have seen such an intensive cultural life and an over-refinement and stylization in etiquette and art. However, the relative peace of that period or the lack of opportunity in the political field might have caused the Javanese, or at least the Javanese courts, to turn their activity inward towards culture and art.

If we return from this excursion into the spirit of this interesting period of Later Mataram's history to the importance of examples, it is natural that in the first place the king himself had to set an example for his people. In the *Serat Rama* exemplary conduct of the king seemed to be prerequisite for an ideal monarch. Setting an example became the duty of a king, and his people would follow his example whether it be "good" or "bad." Thus the king's behavior was a determining factor for the state of affairs in his realm.[116]

Another essential requirement for an ideal ruler was his ability to choose his officers,for which rules were given in many writings. Physical harmony and physical features played an important part in determining the choice.[117] This formed one of the reasons why the *ngelmu firasat* (the

---

112 *Babad Tanah Djawi*, p. 178.
113 De Graaf, "De Regering van Sultan Agoeng," p. 99.
114 Paku Buwana IX, *op. cit.*, pp. 91, 92.
115 Mangkunegara IV, *op. cit.*, p. 41ff. and p. 56ff., in the parts, "Pariwijata" and "Najakawara."
116 Jasadipura I, *op. cit.*, p. 432.
117 Jasadipura I, *op. cit.*, p. 444; Paku Buwana IX, *op. cit.*, p. 180; Mangkunegara IV, *op. cit.*, p. 53; and *Niticastra*, points 30, 106-110.

knowledge to judge character from physiognomy] was always important to the Javanese, although later it was almost exclusively used in gaining knowledge of the character of men.

Such stress on the choice of officials can be readily understood if we see it as a consequence of the close personal ties between master and servant. This also explains another requirement of kingship, that the king must know each of his officials by name. Indeed, until far into the twentieth century, this was considered a noteworthy feature of a member of the indigenous "B.B." ("Binnenlands Bestuur," the Colonial Civil Service) and it was a fact to be proud of if one was personally known or even remembered by a dignitary of high rank.

These writings go into much detail, summing up what one should or should not do. A king is thought particularly un-tactful if he does not give his full confidence to his officers, a very important concept which we will discuss later. A passage in the *Nitiçastra*, however, not found in other writings, says that

> if a king has a character of [indiscriminate] kind-heartedness and resignation, his territory will inevitably be gone, taken away by the enemy.[118]

Another said that a king has to be *adil paramarta* (just and kindhearted); for him there was no "favorite official"[119] because

> there are no differences between children, near relatives, and the common people; if they are serving [the king], all are called *abdi* (servants); if they commit a crime, their punishment will be the same... Since the king has neither kin nor child, relatives nor close relations, not even a favourite wife, only justice is his basic belief.[120]

The *Babad Tanah Djawi* says that the reign of Panembahan Seda Krapjak was *adjeg adil ukumipun, kukuh ing agaminipun* (constant and just in his

118 *Nitiçastra*, p. 61.
119 Paku Buwana IX, *op. cit.*, p. 32.
120 Paku Buwana IV, *op. cit.*, pp. 13, 14. See also: Jasadipura I, *op. cit.*, p. 446.

law, sturdy in his religion).[121] This stresses not only firm religious belief but also justice as an ideal feature of kingship. The Javanese consider Raden Ngabei Rang-gawarsita (1802-1873) the last great *pudjangga*[122] (master of literature); he was a great-grandson of the well-known Jasadipura the Elder (1729-1802) who, with his son Jasadipura the Younger, had contributed much to Javanese literature. Rangga-warsita put the king's task in a comprehensive form in four couplets relating King Kusumawitjitra's advice to *Prabu* (king) Gandakusuma and Djajasusana. The first concern of the king was the organization of administration and the execution of government. His second concern was the control of his officials which must be done in a subtle and unobtrusive manner. The third concern was to know the situation in all parts of the realm in order to be able to give help wherever needed; and the last was to punish wrong-doers or, in other words, to guard the security of the state.[123] This presentation seems quite modern, with its emphasis on administration; the organizational aspect of rule was seen as the foremost task of the king. Of course one can never be sure whether or not Ranggawarsita had been influenced by more modern thought through his acquaintance with Dutch scholars and administrators, among others C. F. Winter and Cohen-Stuart.[124] But again, as the tool to control officials Ranggawarsita recommended the traditional method of secret observation. Furthermore the terms used in these couplets are the traditional ones for expressing matters of rule and government.

Legitimation of Kingship: Succession, Usurpation and the Cult of Glory

In Java kingship is most often made legitimate by proving continuity. A link, whether of blood or of similar experience, with a great predecessor allows a man to partake in the aura of greatness. But also, and this was most important, it makes him a link in the chain of continuity. *Trahing*

---

121 *Babad Tanah Djawi*, p. 113.
122 See also Berg, "Javaansche Geschiedschrijving," Ch. II, par. 6, 7.
123 Tjabang Bagian Bahasa Jogjakarta, *op. cit.*, p. 52, citing the *Witaradya* of R. Ng. Ranggawarsita.
124 Poerbatjaraka, *op.cit.*, pp. 159, 163. Professor Poerbatjaraka's well-founded opinion about the notoriety of Ranggawarsita to incorporate in his writings modern ideas and knowledge which he did not seem to understand adequately makes it necessary to use his writings with caution.

Kusuma, rembesing madu, widjining tapa, tedaking andana warih (descendant of a flower, seepage of honey, seedling of an ascetic, of noble descent),[125] were qualities of a person of august and spotless ancestry. Tracing one's lineage,[126] if possible to a ruling monarch or great vassal,was therefore something on which the Javanese eagerly spent time and effort. The coming of Islam did not eliminate the practice of proving continuity through kinship[127] and it was probably even strengthened by the Arabic custom, followed especially by Javanese of rank, of incorporating one's ancestors' name into one's own name.[128]

When a reigning house was not tied by blood descent to a previous dynasty, the Javanese resorted to various devices to prove continuity. The stories of Ki Ageng Sela's ardent prayers and of Sunan Giri's prophecy that Ki Ageng Pemahahan's descendants would rule Java[129] can perhaps be seen as efforts to make the later kings of Later Mataram legitimate by dint of blood-lineage. Yet, the Javanese sense of reality put a seven generations limit on such a privilege.[130] The houses of Tjirebon and Banten were founded by Fatahillah (also called Faletehan or Sunan Gunung Djati), a foreigner who spread the Islamic faith in the eastern part of West Java. Thus the *babad* writers, faced by the incongruity of two dynasties without ties to a previous ruling House, ingeniously linked them to the old kings of Padjadjaran simply by imagining that a son and a daughter of one of the last Padjadjaran kings had been sent to Arabia. There, the princess, Nji Dalem Satang, married a monarch of Banusrail and bore him a son, Hidajat Sarip, who later returned to Java and became the *wali* Sunan Gunung Djati, the ancestor of the house of Tjirebon.[131]

---

125 Mechelen, "Drie Teksten van Tooneelstukken uit de Wayang Poerwa,"dl. II, p. 13. Said of princess Erawati of Mandraka.

126 H. L. Shorto believes this was an ancient Indonesian practice. Shorto, "A Mon Genealogy of Kings," in D. G. E. Hall, *Historians of Southeast Asia*, London, 1962, p. 67.

127 See also Berg, "Javaansche Geschiedschrijving," p. 96.

128 The demand for continuity is also expressed in the Islamic preoccupation with *isnad*: proof of authenticity and soundness of traditions by citing a chain of authoritative narrators, in Arabic *hadith*.

129 This story was inserted in the *Babad Tanah Djawi*, pp. 36, 68.

130 Strangely enough, even towards the end of the 1940's when the Dutch tried to isolate the young Republic of Indonesia by creating regional *negaras* (states) the story went around that a *negara* head was given by the Dutch government the promise that his descendants — for seven generations — would be regents of a certain regency in East Java.

131 *Babad Tjirebon*, p. 7.

The *Babad Tjirebon*, which contains this story in its most recent form, also tells the story of the division of Mataram (1755) into Surakarta and Jogjakarta and that the Dutch, like the parent of a small child, "spoonfed"[132] the "king of Java." To explain the anomaly of Dutch domination in terms of continuity, the well-known "origin legend" — borrowing Shorto's term[133] — is used; the princess of Padjadjaran with the flaming womb was sold for three guns to the Dutch because of her aberration. She became the mother of the Dutch who were later to come and rule in "Djekarta." Since Djakarta is in the region of West Java, descendants of Padjadjaran had the right of inheritance.[134]

The remarkable similarity of this story to that of Ken Angrok is probably not accidental. Ken Angrok, the first ruler of the Singhasari dynasty, was advised to marry Tunggul Ametung's wife, Ken Dedes, because her flaming womb guaranteed that she would bear future monarchs. The story of the Wandan-woman who restored King Brawidjaja's "health" when he was suffering from *radja singa* (syphilis)[135] is interpreted by Professor Berg as a tale of regeneration.[136] However, it could easily be identified with the former two stories, since, like them, its essence seems to lie in the revitalizing effect of a marriage in order to create an entirely new Ruling House — the Dutch, the Singhasari dynasty, the House of Mataram, respectively. The differences among these founding kings is of course clear, but all are linked in a chain of legitimate succession by their common experience, marriage to a woman endowed with magical revitalizing power.

Continuity could also be expressed in terms of Hinduistic cosmology; the universe is in a state of constant cyclical change. Each cycle is composed of four ever-worsening world-ages (*yugas*).[137] The Javanese of Later Mataram knew this cosmology, although in a corrupted form, and used it to justify dynastic change. The necessity to end the *djaman kalabendu* (the

---

132 *Ibid.*, p. 26.
133 Shorto, *op. cit.*, p. 66.
134 See also: Th. Pigeaud, "Alexander, Sakehder en Sena-pati," *Djawa*, Vol. 7 (1927), nos. 5-6, p. 325.
135 *Babad Mataram*, p. 16.
136 C. C. Berg, "The Islamization of Java," *Studia Islamica* IV (1955), p. 111ff.
137 Heinrich Zimmer, *Myths and Symbols in Indian Art and Civilization*, New York, 1962, pp. 13-17.

Kali-Yuga in Indian mythology, the last and most sinful age in a cycle) in order to enter the era of welfare and prosperity under the *Ratu Adil* (the Just King)[138] was a recurring rationale in the history of revolt and unrest in Java. The principle of patterned continuity has been elaborated in Berg's highly intriguing theory concerning Javanese historical writings.[139] This theory is certainly worthy of careful examination. The idea of an *awatara*, or incarnation (Javanese; *nitis*) of a god, was of course known to the Javanese. Paku Buwana IX placed it, rather awkwardly, in an Islamic context, seeing Sultan Agung as something more than a great king.

> He was the All-Virtuous [that is: God] who had become the king.
> just like the Prophet of Allah in olden times.[140]

Still another example of the effort to wed change to continuity appears in the *Babad Tanah Djawi* and the *Babad Tjirebon* stories about the end of the Hindu kingdoms, Madja-pahit and Padjadjaran. The last kings of these dynasties did not end their existence in this world with physical death in battle against the Moslem forces; they disappeared spiritually and physically (*muksa*). In this way the idea of change was relieved of the banal abruptness of man's work and became colored by the smooth inevitability of God's predestination; change was made more harmonious with the idea of continuity. The *Babad Tjirebon* even provided a device to accomplish this disappearance, the "oil of life" inherited by the Padjadjaran kings from ancient times. Two divine messengers asked the last king of Padjadjaran to return the oil to them; they then smeared it on the rib of a sugar-palm leaf (*sada lanang*). When the rib was planted in the middle of the great square (*alun-alun*), the palace and the king disappeared (*sirna*). It is obvious that the request for the return of the *lenga kahuripan* (oil of life) signified the end of the period of the Hindu kings. At one point in the *wajang* cycle the oil of life became an object of dispute between the Pandawas and Korawas.[141] In the *lakon Pandu-Papa* (Pandu in misery),

---

138 Wiselius, *op. cit.*, pp. 202, 203.
139 See C. C. Berg, *loc. cit.*, and the counter-argument of F. D. K. Bosch, "C. C. Berg and Ancient Javanese History," *Bijdragen*, 112, 1956.
140 Paku Buwana IX, *op. cit.*, p. 92.
141 Mechelen, *Drie en Twintig Teksten*, pp. 117-119, in the *lakon* "Pandu Papa."

Batara Guru, upper-god of the heavens, answers Bratasena's (youth-name of Bima, the second of the Pandawas) question about his deceased father Pandu as follows:

> Your father's soul I have given the 29th Heaven, which will be occupied by all of your descendants, who will die *mikrad* (Arab. ascending to heaven with one's mate-rial body), all your descendants to the time of Madja-pahit. Padjang, Mataram will not be included; those are not my responsibilities.[142]

The finality of the change between Hinduism and Islam is also clearly demonstrated in a *Babad Tjirebon* story in which the divine beings restrained the Padjadjaran monarch from conversion to the Islamic Faith,[143] even though he himself was quite willing. In Madjapahit history, the chasm between Hinduism and Islam is symbolized by the forty days interregnum of Sunan Giri, who — as the foremost *wali* of that time — was able to assure "…that the traces of an unbeliever-king will be entirely eradicated."[144] The forty days interregnum has a special sense of finality since,to the present in Java, a forty day period marks the end of the first phase of commemoration of the dead.

The kingdom of Madjapahit thus came to an end, but kingship itself did not. "At the time of the disappearance of king Brawidjaja, at that very moment, something like an *andaru* (sign of greatness) was seen emerging from the *kraton* of Madjapahit, looking like a streak of lightning, [accompanied by] the frightening sound of thunder, and it fell in Bintara."[145] Bintara is the region where the later kingdom of Demak was located. With this story we come to perhaps the most convincing means of legitimation for the Javanese — the *wahju*, which Pigeaud translates as "godly spirit, force."

In its original Arabic form, *wahy*, it has the meaning of "revelation" from God, but the Javanese thought of it as a substance which graced

---

142 *Ibid.*, p. 119. Observe the precise complementary character of these two stories from sources of different genre — *babad* and *lakon* — which shows a widespread knowledge of such concepts.

143 *Babad Tjirebon*, p. 16.

144 *Babad Tanah Djawi*, p. 30.

145 *Ibid.*

kingship (*wahju kedaton* or *tjahja nurbuwah*),[146] literary genius (*wahju kapudjanggan*), knightly valour (*wahju kapradjuritan*), or *wali*-ship and even *bupati*-ship. This god-given substance was not always granted to a specific person, as was seen in the transfer of kingship from Madjapahit to Demak. It was visualized in different shapes and forms — bright luminescence, a "star," but most often it was seen as a dazzling blue, green or white ball of light (*andaru, pulung*), streaking through the night sky.[147] In the popular *lakon Wahju Tjakraningrat*, the young *ksatrias* of the Pandawa and Kurawa clans and the crown-prince of Dwarawati compete in ascetic practice and abstinence in order to attract the *wahju*. In the lakon the *wahju* is pictured as a divine being. Thus the descendants of Ardjuna's son, Abimanju, were assured of Java's throne for all time to come. A passage in the *Babad Tanah Djawi*[148] tells a story of the *pangeran dipati (anom)* (crown-prince), later Amangkurat II, from which we might conclude that the *wahju* was actually seen as *the* substance of great power and ability. After Trunadjaja's occupation of Mataram's capital, Amangkurat I fled with the crown prince and later died in exile. The prince was firmly convinced that instead of trying to regain what he had lost to the rebels he should go on pilgrimage to the Holy Land. He was unresponsive to the pleas of his *bupatis* to relinquish his plan until in a dream he saw a *wahju* in the form of seven moons and a "child as small as a kris-handle, shining like the sun" entering his body. He then completely changed his mind and decided to fight for his lost kingdom. His followers

> …did not recognize their master; formerly his face was drawn and without expression, now his countenance became bright and of a stately gravity.[149]

It is noteworthy that such signs of legitimacy appeared in the *Babad*

---

146 *Ibid.*, p. 174.
147 Similarly, the Javanese perceive of epidemic diseases as dripping red balls of light (the *teluh bradja*). The "presents" exchanged by the spirit-queen of the Indian Ocean, Njai Lara Kidul, and the spirit-guardians of Mount Lawu and Mount Kelud in Java are also seen as *pulungs* which entered into the crater or the sea with a mighty boom.
148 *Babad Tanah Djawi*, respectively pp. 36, 76, 30, and *Babad Mataram*, p. 27.
149 *Babad Tanah Djawi*, p. 174.

Tanah Djawi mostly in stories of usurpation. *Wahju* is first mentioned in the story of Padjang's assumption of Demak's power through its first as well as last monarch Djaka Tingkir, later Sultan Adiwidjaja. *Wahju* next plays a role when Panembahan Senapati usurped the Padjang throne, and again when Pangeran Puger, later Paku Buwana I, with the help of the V.O.C., forceably expelled his nephew Sunan Amangkurat Mas (Amangkurat III) from his capital in 1705. All these cases show that legitimation proven by possession of the *wahju* was final and not to be doubted since it clearly came from God himself. In the last case, that of Pangeran Puger, the argument for legitimacy was further strengthened by the principle of regeneration, not much different from the symbolism of the princess with the flaming womb, but now in a more undisguised form.[150] The *Babad Tanah Djawi* relates:

> The story was told that the [deceased, namely Amang-kurat II] king's manhood stood erect and on top of it was a glittering shine only the size of a grain of pepper. But nobody observed it. Only Pangeran Puger saw it. Pangeran Puger quickly sipped up the light ...and the manhood ceased to stand erect. It was God's will that Pangeran Puger should succeed to the throne.[151]

A *wahju* left the king at his death — or at his apparent downfall — to go over to those chosen by the gods. It should be realized that the device of divine sanction in the form of a *wahju* made kingship extremely vulnerable, open to illegal change. But such change was only a change of personnel and never a change in the concept of kingship itself. For, regardless of his previous status, the moment the usurper assumed the position of king, he was automatically emblazoned with all the traditional attributes of kingship which he could not dispose of in preference to another system of government, unless he wanted to be accused of an unkingly attitude.

---

150 Professor Hoesein Djajadiningrat in his dissertation is of the opinion that the stories woven around the figure of Pangeran Puger were obviously meant to justify his usurpation and this led him to the conclusion that this part of the *Babad Tanah Djawi* had been written by contemporaries or at least by persons living not too far after the period described, a fact which, with due caution, make these *babads* "or parts of them" usable as *historical sources*. (Hoesein Djajadiningrat, *op. cit.*, pp. 241, 307.)

151 *Babad Tanah Djawi*, p. 260.

He had to leave everything as it was and comply with established customs for the sake of harmony and continuity. Paku Buwana IV (1788-1820) readily agreed that his ancestors had lived the life of the common peasant, but of course in his august position it was difficult to admit his low origin. He explains this therefore with the words that

> ...the life-rule of the ancestors was that of a life of humbleness. That was what they used to disguise their ascetic life. Their asceticism was screened by living as peasants; this was what was used as a cover, with the purpose that it should not be seen by all, ...their humility contained a deep meaning.[152]

Paku Buwana IV's explanation in fact emphasized the great difference between the *kawula* and the *gusti*. In connection with the idea of usurpation this means that the character of kingship could not be changed, even if the usurper came directly from the people, because then he simply could no longer be identified as *kawula*.

The ritual of enthronement as part of the legitimation of kingship naturally has its own significance. However, sources describing enthronement of kings are not easily found and Javanese literature itself does not give elaborate accounts. A ceremony is described several times in the *Babad Tanah Djawi* and once in the *wajang-lakons*, which in its crude primitiveness seems to have importance in terms of legitimation. The *Babad Tanah Djawi* describes the investiture of Panembahan Seda Krapjak (1601-1613): after the death of Panembahan Senapati, on a Monday (Mondays and Thursdays are the days of audience), two trusted dignitaries of the late king, Adipati Mandaraka and Senapati's younger brother, Pan-geran Mangkubumi, took the crown prince by his hands, standing at his left and right side, and led him to the *sitinggil* (the open audience hall built on artificially raised ground). After seating the crown prince on the golden stool (*dampar kentjana*), Mangkubumi arose and announced in a loud voice:

> All people of Mataram, whoever they be, witness, that at this

---

152 Paku Buwana IV, *op. cit.*, p. 37.

very day, the crown-prince assumes the sultanship,succeeding his august father. If there is anybody who feels dissatisfied in his heart, show your intention now and I will be your opponent in duel.

At this the people of Mataram *asaur peksi djumurung* (hailed it unanimously).[153] The last part of the proclamation, especially the so-called *panantang* (challenge) by the king's champions with its obvious appeal to the use of force, is of a rather primitive character, which might indicate the great age of this custom. The ceremony falls into two distinct parts, the proclamation of the enthronement and the acceptance by the congregation of high dignitaries and other important persons at the audience. This ceremony was even carried out by the Dutch at the installation of the *susuhunans* of Surakarta or the sultans of Jogjakarta when the Dutch themselves acted as champions of the new king. At the investiture of Hamengku Buwana III in 1792, the Dutch Governor representing his government but also acting as champion of the candidate asked the *Lurah Sentana* (Chief of the Royal Clan) and the *Kepala Bupati* (Headman of the Bupatis) whether they were *gilig* (in perfect unanimity) with the enthronement. He was answered with the traditional agreement.[154] Curiously, in a *wajang-lakon*, when Pandu, the father of the Pandawas, is initiated as king in Ngastina, the investiture is proclaimed by Semar, the *panakawan* with divine characteristics.[155] One is tempted to deduce from these stories that the essence of this ceremony must be legitimation of kingship by acceptance, or, more accurately, by the submission of the whole population represented by the audience at the throne-hall. The role of Semar as king's champion in the *wajang* story may indicate that the *panantang*, the challenge, had changed from its original meaning, a show of force, to the sanction of God, here personified in Semar. On the other hand, Semar's role may be explained by the fact that he was the oldest and the most venerated in the realm, for, when the *panantang* at the enthronement of Amangkurat II was omitted, the *adipati* of Sampang

---

153 *Babad Tanah Djawi*, p. 113. See also pp. 117, 141, 278. The *Babad Tanah Djawi* in poetic metre has another ver-sion of the ceremony (*Babad Tanah Djawi*, ed. Balai Poestaka, Batavia, 1939, Vol. 7, pp. 74, 75).

154 C. Poensen, "Amangkoe Boewana II (Sepoeh)," *Bijdragen*, Vol. 58, 1905, p. 81.

155 J. van der Vliet, "Pandoe," *Bijdragen*, Vol. 27 (1879), p. 228.

commented that the oldest relative of the late king should have installed the crown prince.[156] The complete attendance of the clergy and other personages of religious fame, which seems to have been required at these ceremonies, undoubtedly served to strengthen the authority of the king in the realms of religion and belief.[157] Officially, their attendance was called for to *ngestreni* (to honor by one's presence) the investiture.

Such means of legitimation as royal descent and the mark of divine consent (e.g., the *wahju*) served another and far more important purpose in the realities of state-life. They became most important political devices for enhancing the king's *kawibawan* (authority). For since he was the central, all-dominating and sole source of power in the state, his major concern had to be upholding authority, and he did so by continuously demonstrating his greatness. Glorifying the king was made particularly necessary by Javanese cosmology which identified the greatness of the king with the greatness of the whole kingdom. And, politically speaking, the greater glory of the king is equated with greater prestige and authority. There must not be anything which could challenge the king's greatness and it was significant that the greatness of the king in Javanese literature, especially in the *wajang*, was always measured against the amount of respect shown him by *other* rulers. A great state was one which was *dawa kuntjarane, unggul kawibawane* (far-reaching is its fame, high is its prestige), or in other words, *gede obore, padang djagade, duwur kukuse, adoh kuntjarane* (great is its torch, radiant is its realm, high-rising its smoke, far-reaching its fame); it was respected by other states.[158] The *radja sewu nagara*, or "the kings of the thousand states," who attended and affirmed the investiture of the father of the Pandawas as king of Ngastina attested to the unsurpassed greatness of Pandu Dewanata as an example of the ideal world-ruler.[159]

The dependent relationship between the realm and the person of the king meant that the king's benevolence penetrated the whole kingdom.[160] Many incidents are related in Javanese literature in which the state of

---

156 *Babad Tanah Djawi*, ed. Balai Poestaka, Vol. 16, pp. 43, 44. The version in poetic metres.
157 *Ibid.*, Vol. 21, p. 17. See also *Babad Tanah Djawi*, ed. Meinsma, pp. 278,340.
158 Mechelen, "Drie Teksten," p. 1.
159 Van der Vliet, *op. cit.*, p. 228.
160 See p. 36 .

mind of a hero, and especially a monarch, and then to a far greater extent because of his extraordinary powers, is reflected in or even affects nature. This is especially dramatic in the *lakon* relating Wrekudara's search in the forest for the highest truth.[161] When Paku Buwana IX lost his queen, he felt that the whole kingdom reflected his despondent mood, "cold in their hearts, the whole kingdom is plunged into sadness."[162]

It is understandable that such an emphasis on the king's greatness inevitably led to systematic efforts towards glorification of the person of the king. The Cult of Glory became the most substantial and effective means of enhancing authority. This is seen in the description of the king as *ratu gung binatara* (the great divine king)[163] and in the phrases *banda-bandu* (rich in material wealth as well as relatives) and also in the well-known phrase in ancient Indian political thinking, *mbaudenda njakrawati* (with the power to punish and a ruler of the whole world).[164] Two kinds of tools were available to the Cult of Glory, one which was of an immaterial, or abstract character, and the other of a more perceptible and concrete character. The tools are however not as distinct as they seem at first glance. Both are expressions of the macro/micro-cosmos relationship which made kingship a replica of godly rule, giving it a two-sided aspect of spiritual as well as material excellence. For the Javanese saw the godly realms as a place of superfluous riches, a place of ultimate greatness in terms of material as well as spiritual wealth. Thus, the earthly king also had to seek his glory in these two categories.

Probably the most important of the spiritual tools to glory was religious merit or spiritual merit in general. Possessing the characteristics, conduct and behavior required of an ideal king most increased a king's glory. Such spiritual perfection was thought to be demonstrated by the possessor's capacity to perform feats which no ordinary human being could perform (*sekti*). A striking story in this connection is of Sultan Agung's switch, after his failure to conquer Batavia in 1628 and 1629, from the quest for

---

161 Prijohoetomo, *Nawaruci*, Groningen, 1934, p. 162 (Bima-sutji Canto VII, Strophe 7-10).
162 Paku Buwana IX, *op. cit.*, p. 23 in the part "Gandrung Turida."
163 See also the *Babad Tanah Djawi*, p. 117. It says of Sultan Agung: *ratu ageng, ambek adil paramarta* (a great king, just and kindhearted).
164 See also H. C. Humme, *Abiåså*, 's-Gravenhage, 1878, p. 30, where the word *njakrawati* is also used.

greatness on the battlefield to that of intense religious endeavour.[165] The might and splendour of religious monuments too had always occupied a major place in enhancing the king's glory,although in the Later Mataram period nothing was built which could match the great structures of the Old Javanese period. Nevertheless, we can detect this idea on a much lesser scale in the Mataram kings' veneration and occasional restoration of the Demak mosque.[166] The building of a rather small *pendapa* (open hall) at the holy graves of Tembajat by Sultan Agung served the same purpose.[167] Actually the king's *kraton* (palace) in the vastness and splendour of its design and con-struction and the royal graves at Imagiri were in themselves tokens of the king's glory.[168]

Another means of enhancing royal glory was the king's genealogical tree. The more august persons, real or legendary, it incorporated and the further back it went, the greater the king's prestige. The Javanese mind strove to syncretize the two different cultures of Hindu religion and Islam in order to establish the desired continuity; the kings of Mataram were therefore provided with a double genealogy, the *Sedjarah Pangiwa* (the left history) and the *Sedjarah Panengen* (the right history).[169] According to Berg these genealogies were first composed only in the Later Mataram period.[170] Islam had forced the replacement of the Old Javanese king-god identification. Consequently, the genealogies were forged in order to maintain a resemblance to the king-god identification; it was irrelevant that all standards of chronology or the consequences of places and events were ignored. The Right Genealogy began with the Prophet Mohammad, in the *Babad Mataram* called Kandjeng Rasul, followed by (among others) a princess of Tjempa (Champa) and her son Raden Rachmat,[171] the later Sunan Ngampel, oldest and most prominent of the *walis*. It probably then continued with Pangeran Pekik of Surabaja, who married Sultan Agung's sister and whose daughter bore the later Amangkurat III of Mataram. Amangkurat III ended the line of kings from this Right Genealogy.

---

165 De Graaf, *Geschiedenis van Indonesië*, pp. 109, 113.
166 *Babad Tanah Djawi*, p. 306.
167 De Graaf, "De Regering van Sultan Agung," p. 202.
168 De Graaf, "Titels en Namen," p. 77.
169 Djajadiningrat, *op. cit.*, p. 298.
170 Berg, "Javaansche Geschiedschrijving," p. 96.
171 *Babad Mataram*, Vol. I, p. l0ff.

But there must have been another link connecting later Mataram kings with the *Sedjarah Panengen*.[172] The *Sedjarah Pangiwa* went further in its genealogical extravagance. Beginning with Nabi Adam and Nabi Sis (Adam and Seth), names of Islamic origin, it then went through the Hindu pantheon, then through the legendary king Watugunung of indigenous origin to the ancestors of the Pandawas, epic figures from the Indian *Mahabharata*. It continued with the first king of Java, king Swela Tjala of Purwatjarita (a name denoting nothing in particular as it simply means "the beginning of the story," so referring to antiquity in general). Then came a jumble of names of kings, historical ones like those of Koripan, Djenggala and Kediri, Galuh, and Singhasari, but in the wildest disorder. The genealogy then listed a connection with Padjadjaran in West Java, then with Madjapahit in the East and through a link in Palembang to the Sultans of Demak where it came to an end. Through another branch of descendants of Madjapahit's last king Brawidjaja, via the story of the Wandan woman[173] and the popular *Kyageng Tarub* story involving a celestial nymph, the genealogy came at last to the first kings of Mataram.[174] Thus the kings of Mataram were bedecked with an ancestry which included divine personages as well as famous personalities from all known countries of all times, for the sake of their glory and so for their prestige and authority.

A fourth means of glorification was the king's alignment with what the indigenous world of belief had to offer in magical and spiritual powers. The well-known Naga-princess in Khmer myth, as a symbol of the fertility of the soil, consummated marriage with the kings at certain times to assure the welfare of the country.[175] Java also had its spirit-queen, the mighty and ever-beautiful Njai Lara Kidul, ruler of the spirit world of the Segara Kidul (the Indian Ocean), much feared by the Javanese because of the toll in human lives which she levied from time to time from the adjacent coastal regions of Java. So a Javanese king, if he did not want to lose his prestige, had to subject the goddess to his authority, and what better means of alignment could the Javanese think of than that of

---

172   The links to the Mataram House in this genealogy are not clear to the writer.
173   See p. 54.
174   *Babad Tanah Djawi*, p. 24ff.
175   D. G. E. Hall, *History of Southeast Asia*, London, 1955 p. 24.

marriage. Njai Lara Kidul married first Panembahan Senapati[176] and later all the kings of Mataram, thereby assuring the safety of the realm, for in times of distress she would come to the king's aid with her innumerable spirit-armies. But, from time to time, feminine unpredictability still made her take the lives of the king's subjects in epidemics! The yearly ceremony of the *labuh*, the sending of gifts on a raft into the Indian Ocean by the rulers of Jogjakarta, attested to the bond between the rulers of the human world and Njai Lara Kidul, the queen of the spirit world. Gifts were also offered to the spirit-guardian of Mount Lawu.

The function of the *kotang Antakusuma* (the Antakusuma-jacket) can perhaps be incorporated into this fourth category of means of royal glorification.[177] This relic, a *pusaka* (holy object of inheritance) is in the possession of the Sultans of Jogjakarta and is worn by them only in the danger of battle. According to Hooykaas, the *kotang* is a symbol of the king as the cosmic ruler, for while wearing it the king can stand between the earth and the Underworld or between earth and the Heavens. Hooykaas identifies the jacket with the skin of the Snake-king (the ruler of the underworld) and also with the rainbow which in folk belief forms the bridge to Heaven. The idea of a bridge to Heaven is said to be of indigenous origin and widely known throughout Southeast Asia. It has also found a place in Javanese Islamic tradition. In this tradition Sunan Kalidjaga is said to have made the *Kotang Antakusuma* from a goatskin which had contained another Kotang Antakusuma and a letter from the Prophet saying that he himself had worn the jacket. This goatskin bundle fell amidst the synod of *walis* in Demak.[178] The jacket subsequently made from the goatskin was first named Kyai Gundil (the Hairless) and later became one of Jogjakarta's *pusakas* under the name Kotang Antakusuma. This legend again reveals the Javanese desire to incorporate all significant Javanese beliefs into the new culture of Islam, thus providing it with appropriate accoutrements for the jacket, which allowed the king to associate himself with the denizens of the three worlds, again raising him far beyond the average human capacity.

---

176 *Babad Tanah Djawi*, p. 79.
177 Jacoba Hooykaas, "The Rainbow in Ancient Indonesian Religion," *Bijdragen*, 112, 1956, pp. 291-322.
178 *Babad Mataram*, p. 62. The *Babad Tanah Djawi* (p. 103) has a slightly different version.

With the Kotang Antakusuma we come to the fifth category of non-material means of glorification, the *pusakas* (holy relics of inheritance). Their importance lay in the magical powers they were thought to contain. Between a *pusaka* and a magically powerful person, like the king, there exists a mutually stimulating effect. For each kris (an intrinsically powerful object), for instance, there is an appropriate wearer;[179] thus, a person might not be "strong" enough to own a particular kris because it should be worn only by a king (*ageming ratu*). On the other hand, a king may be so powerful that, for instance, his carriage of state also becomes "strong," an object of reverence. Water used to wash such a carriage at certain times was and is much coveted for its power to restore youth and vigor.[180]

The *pusakas* include a wide variety of objects and the origins assigned them by tradition were also varied. The famous "crown of Madjapahit," lost in the Trunadjaja war and rediscovered by the Dutch at the fall of the rebels1 stronghold in Kediri and then returned to Amangkurat II, had seemed to be lost forever. As we have seen, the Demak mosque and Sunan Kalidjaga's tomb are also considered *pusakas*.[181] Another *pusaka*, the war-gong Kyai Bitiak, was made a *pusaka* by the consent of Sunan Kalidjaga.[182] However, the majority are weapons, primarily krisses and lances although more modern weapons like the two cannons, Kyai and Njai Setomi of Surakarta's kings, are also considered *pusakas*. One kris was made by the famous smith-sage (*empu*) Supa of Tuban, and was named Kandjeng Kyai Sengkelat. Others were traced through a long line of inheritance, like the lance Kyai Plered;[183] still others were taken from the enemy such as the lance Kyai Baruklinting, which was thought to have been the tongue of a huge *naga* doing *tapa* (ascetic practice). This lance was connected with the well-loved story about the *Kyageng* of Mangir[184] who dared to stand up against Mataram because he possessed the lance. The Javanese have woven a romantic story around this uprising, the authenticity of which we will leave untested. Another *pusaka* is the *gamelan* (complete set of instruments composing the Javanese orchestra) Njai Sekati.

---

179 Rassers, *op. cit.*, p. 224.
180 Kandjeng Kyai Garuda Yaksa, Jogjakarta's state-coach, was made in a European country.
181 See p. 32.
182 *Babad Tanah Djawi*, p. 44. Two rings were also *pusakas*; *ibid.*, p. 60 .
183 *Babad Tanah Djawi*, p. 27.
184 Kyageng is a title given to persons respected for their devotion to the religious life.

In terms of magical power, aside from these lifeless — from the rationalist Western point of view — objects, we can include the custom of having magically powerful persons at court with the same objective as that of the *pusakas* mentioned above. Artisans, who exercise "dangerous" occupations like silver-, copper-, gold-, and blacksmiths, potters, *dalangs*, and managers of dancing girls were included in this category be-cause of the forces they worked with[185] (fire, passion, the power of impersonation). The *empus*, the weapon-smiths, were granted particularly high esteem.[186] The *Babad Mataram* relates that at one time King Brawidjaja of Madjapahit gathered all the *empus* in the palace to make him a particular type of kris, which would be used as a *tumbal* (exorcizing object to ward off bad luck) for the realm. One by one the names of all the *empus* are mentioned which indicates their revered position in society.[187] Another source of magical power seemed to be the *palawidjas*, dwarfs, blind men, albinos, etc., who because of congenital physical deformities were considered to have "dangerous" forces in them. Some of them were kept close to the king, not only to neutralize their harmful influences[188] upon the community of common men, but mainly because these influences, to the magically forceful king, would become a stimulating and enhancing rather than endangering force.

Wealth must be considered one of the material means of the Cult of Glory. This included a large population and a large number of kin. Numerous kin gave the king more strength in terms of support,and,in a society where close relations formed an essential element in the social framework, relatives, by virtue of the natural ties of blood, constituted the basic relationship-group, much stronger and much more closely knit than they are now. This is shown in Ki Ageng Pemanahan's words, when he explained his plan to Sultan Adiwidjaja of Padjang to dispose of Arya Penangsang of Djipang:

Would Your Majesty please look from afar only. I myself with all my kinsmen will meet him in battle.[189]

---

185 Pigeaud, *Javaanse Volksvertoningen*, p. 58.
186 See for the important position of the *empu*: Rassers, *op. cit.*, p. 224.
187 *Babad Mataram*, p. 79.
188 Pigeaud, *Javaanse Volksvertoningen*, p. 58.
189 *Babad Tanah Djawi*, p. 54. This took place in or about 1570.

A large population meant that the king had sufficient men to extract wealth from the soil and to form the mass-armies of fighting men as well as equipment-bearers which were reported by Dutch envoys. Two thousand armed men could be gathered within half a day by sounding the war-gongs and, later, by firing the cannon Kyai Guntur Geni (Thunder of Fire) in the capital.[190] In the *wajang*, when Jamawidura, uncle of the Pandawas, was granted the rather insignificant region of Tjarang Glagah (Spiked Branches and Reeds), he expressed his desire for a large population:

Perhaps later it will become a large city, if only it will become populated.[191]

Perhaps when the Mataram rulers moved large numbers of the population from the conquered regions to Mataram proper[192] it was considered a means of enhancing the king's greatness. If one knew exactly how many conquered peoples were forced to move and how and where they were given lands it might be possible to decide whether these measures were taken purely for economic reasons or whether they also had political significance .

The king's armed forces provided a further material tool of Glory. In Later Mataram the army consisted of a specially picked body of men, the king's guard, incorporating several units with their own names, specific weapons and assigned duties. Most of them were guardsmen stationed at certain places in the palace-compound, but they also acted as executors of death sentences. The guard consisted of both infantrymen and mounted troops.[193] The forces of Sultan Sepuh and of Surakarta were reduced to virtual extinction following the new contracts with the English in August 1812 and Sultan Sepuh's failure to shake off the yoke of foreign rule.[194] The troops of the Kraton of Surakarta then consisted of 29 units, from

---

190 De Graaf, "De Regering van Sultan Agung," p. 125.
191 Van der Vliet, *op. cit.*, p. 328.
192 De Graaf, "De Regering van Sultan Agung," p. 263.
193 Soemantri mentioned 3 units of mounted troops, which did not exist anymore at his time. (Soemantri Hardjo-dibroto (trans.), "De Wijzigingen der gebruiken en gewoonten aan het Solosche Hof," in *Djawa*, Vol. 11 (1931), no. 4, p. 164.)
194 Sultan Sepuh was Amangku Buwana II (1792-1810, 1811-1812, 1826-1828). Veth, *op. cit.*, Vol. II, p. 586.

15 to 125 men strong. One corps, the Martalulut, executed the death sentence by the kris, sabre or lance; another, the Singanagara, executed the death penalty by decapitation and the penalty of mutilation of hand or foot. This was done with the *wedung* (short, broad knife).[195] At various periods reigning monarchs had formed these corps, the oldest of which was reputedly the Tamtama, formed during the Demak-period around 1500 A.D.[196] It is related that Ki- Djaka Tingkir was made its commander under Sultan Trenggana (1521-1546) when he showed his extraordinary abilities by jumping backwards over a pond from a sitting position.[197] At that time, in order to join this special unit one had to possess *kadigdajan* (magical physical powers, like invulnerability to weapons) which consisted of the ability to crack the skull of an enraged wild bull (*banteng*) with one's bare fist. These stories were undoubtedly created to illustrate the extraordinary capacities of the Tamtama. At that time, also, the units seem to have been much larger, for Sultan Trenggana intended to enlarge the Tamtama corps by four hundred. Apart from their duty as bodyguards to the king, these special corps might have also formed the core of the army to be sent into battle.[198] They were supplemented by the common peasantry, recruited through a general levy (*kerigan*).[199] This levy provided not only the fighting men but also, and perhaps for the greater part, manpower to carry or haul the necessary equipment and supplies.[200] The basic characteristic of the army lay, however, in the closely knit cores of trusted followers of the commander (the king, a *bupati* or some other dignitary). These special units earned their exceptional position as much as the trusted followers of the king as for their martial ability. This was demonstrated by the careers of two men who rose to the highest rank, namely Madjapahit's able *patih Gadjah* Mada, a former commander of the Bhayangkari guards, and Ki Djaka Tingkir, the later Sultan Adiwidjaja and son-in-law of the Sultan of Demak, who began as commanding officer of the elite corps of the Tamtama. The relationship of trust and loyalty between master and follower, between *gusti* and *kawula*,

195 *Babad Tanah Djawi*, pp. 132, 304.
196 C. F. Winter, Senior, *Javaansche Zamenspraken*, Amsterdam, 1862, pp. 25-29.
197 *Babad Tanah Djawi*, p. 37.
198 *Ibid.*, pp. 57, 106.
199 *Ibid.*, p. 160. See also: Jasadipura I, *op. cit.*, p. 294.
200 *Ibid.*, p. 297.

was demonstrated by Tumenggung Danupaja. On hearing that his lord Pangeran Alit had died in a fruitless effort to wrest the Mataram throne from Amangkurat II (1677-1703), Danupaja ended his life by taking-poison.[201] And, on the other hand, the *Babad Tanah Djawi* frequently tells of how a successful cam-paign was followed by the soldiers' immediate reward with rank and goods.[202]

The close relationship between leader and trusted followers made the army a ready and willing tool for use in the Cult of Glory, because sharing in greatness, psychologically perhaps more than materially, formed a strong stimulus for the soldier. Glory was eagerly pursued through the roads of war, because even the threatening presence of a strong army ensured a submissive attitude from neighboring countries, and thus the glory of the king and his followers was enhanced. In the *Babad Tanah Djawi* the order to subjugate a region or city appears to be given so casually that one must conclude that warfare — which of course in itself did not have the widely devastating effect that it has now — was a usual affair.[203] Some examples will illustrate this point. Sultan Agung at one time ordered Tumenggung Suratani:

> Go and attack the Eastern part of the realm. Take all the troops and all my kinsmen with you, try them out on the battlefield[204]

without any further explanation. At another time it is narrated:

> Not long afterwards His Majesty the King gave the order to besiege Surabaja

also without any comment as to the reason for the attack.[205] Giving reasons for the expeditions does not seem to have been considered necessary. In two instances in the *Babad Tanah Djawi* where a reason is given, they are

---

201 *Ibid.*, p. 145.
202 *Ibid.*, pp. 120, 185, 301.
203 See also: de Jonge, *op. cit.*, Vol. IV, p. 58, where it was told of Sultan Agung that one could not meet him in the months of April, May or October, because he would then be in the field leading his troops on some expedition.
204 *Babad Tanah Djawi*, p. 118.
205 *Ibid.*, p. 129. See also pp. 135, 140.

the same, namely that the opponent was not willing to submit (*nungkul*) and recognize the suzerainty of Mataram's rulers.[206] In fact, in the Cult of Glory this proved to be *the* valid reason for war. When the *dalang* says that the surrounding countries subjected themselves to the sovereignty of a great king without resorting to war it is expressed picturesquely in the words *kang tjedak manglung, kang tebih tumijung* (the closer ones lowered their tops [like bamboo] the farther ones leaned over [like a palmtree in a strong wind]). This description only affirms the fact that warfare was the usual method to assure submission. Such a mechanical, almost inevitable tendency towards expansion (*ngelar djadjahan*: expanding one's territorial jurisdiction) is clearly found in the *mandala*-idea in ancient Indian political thinking.[207] Although it is not certain that this idea was known in the Later Mataram period, the final result of such a policy — the king as world ruler (Skrt: *chakravarttin*) — was certainly not unknown to the Javanese who used the word *njakrawati*, as we have seen above.[208] Clearly, Sultan Agung's intention to work towards his ideal of rebuilding the empire of Madja-pahit[209] was not very different. It was therefore only natural that a passage in the inexhaustible *Babad Tanah Djawi* should show, at the time of Panembahan Senapati, the fear of the regional power-holders in Eastern Java that such an inevitable expansion would follow the gradual rise of Mataram. Therefore, sometime about 1590, the Panembahan of Madiun, an influential regional head, gathered

...the bupatis of the Eastern territories [East Java], who were not yet subject to Mataram, to plan an attack on the capital of Mataram,

---

206 *Ibid.*, pp. 112, 134.

207 The *mandala* (circle, namely of influence, interest or ambitions) can be described as a complex of geopolitical relations, relating to boundaries and to contact with foreign countries. The doctrine emphasizes the cult of expansion, a necessary spur to the struggle for existence, self-assertion and world domination, and the dynamic factor calculated to disturb the equilibrium of inter-state relations. A state's belligerence is in the first place directed towards its closest neighbor(s), thus making necessary the friendship of the state next to the foe, which, because of its proximity, is also a natural enemy of the foe. But if the mutual foe should be conquered, the two allies would become close neighbors, which of necessity would create a new enmity. So this circle of alignment and alienation would steadily expand until a universal peace is reached by the establishment of a world-state with a sole and supreme ruler (chakravarttin). (See further: Benoy Kumar Sarkar, *Creative India*, Lahore, 1937.)

208 Page 62.

209 Berg, "Islamization of Java," p. 125f.

because Senapati could be compared to a fire the size of a firefly's. It was better to put it out with water as soon as possible, so that it would not spread into a conflagration.[210]

The *bupatis* agreed.

The last of the material means for the Cult of Glory was material wealth as such. And here again the basic idea of richness and splendor lay in visualizing the king's environment as a replica of the heavenly abodes, of the Kaendran (Indra's Heaven) or even of the Suralaja, the abode of the highest deity, Batara Guru. The *dalang* describes the splendor and beauty displayed when the king comes out to hold audience, including the young maidens who bear the *upatjara* (the regalia of kingship). He ends with a comparison:

> strong was the fragrance of the king penetrating far outside beyond the *pangurakan* (the entrance to the great square); gone were his human features and he looked like the deity Batara Sambu, attended by a host of nymphs.[211]

In the palace, the entrances to the inner chambers and the pleasure garden were made in imitation of the entrance to Suralaja, the two guardian giants, Tjingkara and Bala Upata, here represented as statues. The *dalang* relates that in the inner courtyard

> as gravel to cover the yard *nila-* and *pakadj* a stones [kinds of semi-precious stones] were used and when they were raked by the feet of the many passing serving-maidens they shone and glittered like so many shooting stars.[212]

This display of wealth was apparent also in the preference for gold (paint) and in the pomp and grandeur of the court ceremonies. Thus, with regard to earthly wealth the king had also to display an unsurpassable lavishness.

---

210 *Babad Tanah Djawi*, p. 100.
211 Mechelen, "Drie Teksten," p. 2.
212 *Ibid.*, p. 2 5.

When considering the Cult of Glory, one is apt to conclude that the main purposes of kingship in Java lay in the pursuit of the king's glorification alone, and the practice of state-craft lent credibility to such a point of view. However, in the context of Javanese ideals and cosmology, kingship, as a reflection of God's rule, is the maintenance of harmony and order in this smaller world of man, and thus such a lofty task, such a position of high honor, could not have so insignificant a purpose as the acquisition of earthly wealth or physical power or any other outward sign of greatness *alone*. In Javanese tradition material wealth *per se* has never been a purpose of life. The words *agung* or *luhur* (literally: "great" and "high") always had the connotation of an inner greatness and perfection, the true signs of the greatness of a king. Submission to a really great king could never therefore be the result of war but had to be a response to the king's noble and wise rule, to quote the *dalang's* words:

> Many kingdoms have submitted of their own free will without being subjugated by force; it is only because they are overwhelmed by the king's character.[213]

Attachment to wealth was considered an ignoble attitude. Although a king, because of his inner magnitude, must be bestowed with riches, fortunes, like his benevolence, must also flow out from the king to the benefit of whomever might need it. This was why *dana* or beneficence was thought of as the most important feature of a kingly attitude. In the *Asta Brata*,[214] the characteristic of the ideal king mentioned first is dana, attributed to the most prominent of the God Guru's sons, Endra. In the *wajang, dana* again is mentioned first by the puppeteer in describing the good character of the king[215] and is repeated last:

> for certain, one cannot measure the beneficent gifts of His Majesty the King of Mandaraka.[216]

---

213 Tjan Tjoe Siem, *Hoe Koeroepati zich zijn vrouw verwerft*, Leiden, 1938, p.4.
214 See p. 43.
215 Mechelen, "Drie Teksten," p. 1.
216 *Ibid.*, p. 2.

So display of magical power, physical might and material wealth formed an essential part, a necessary decoration, of kingship but *only* as the consequences of the king's inner magnanimity; the king's virtue is proven by his use of these abundant resources.

It was the king's use of the signs of greatness which the Javanese keenly observed. Misuse of his powers was seen as a sign that his greatness was waning and that his downfall was at hand. Javanese tolerate oppression when they think the king "is still bestowed with the *wahju*" (*lagi kewahjon*) for it is of no use whatsoever to remonstrate against the possessor of the *wahju*. Moreover, since such behavior is the unmistakable sign that the *wahju* will soon leave the king, his ruin is consolingly inevitable. The downfall of a holder of power was thus seen, like any and all events, to be part of the cosmic order; man can take no deliberate part, for when he does act, he is merely a tool in the hands of Providence.

Signs of the downfall of a king were varied. The *Babad Tanah Djawi* described the fall of Amangkurat I (1645-1677) as follows:

> At that time His Majesty's behaviour was different from what it usually was; he often punished severely, and continuously indulged himself in cruelties. His *bupatis*, *mantris* (officials) and kin were very uncertain of their position and order had deteriorated very badly. All the Mataram people felt fear in their hearts; sun-and moon-eclipses occurred frequently; rain was falling out of season; a comet was seen every night. Ash-rain and earthquakes [occurred]. Many omens were seen. These were signs that the kingdom was facing ruin.[217]

The *Babad Mataram* speaks of an "old" state with many "nuisances"; many became enemies "not fearing or obeying their king."[218] Wibisana, in the *Serat Rama*, on seeing the signs of destruction, told his brother Dasamuka (Rawana) that

---

217 *Babad Tanah Djawi*, p. 154.
218 *Babad Mataram*, Vol. V, p. 15.

animals of the forest have sought refuge in the city …their sight has changed. Ngalengka is seen as a forest, and with great noise the animals enter the town, the birds give wailing cries; it is clear [that the city] will be destroyed.[219]

Professor Schrieke pointed out that in older Javanese literature a king's drunkenness and an ill-mannered attitude towards people of religion were seen as tokens of a *pralaja*, the period of destruction.[220] That drunkenness was also considered a sign of *pralaja* in the Later Mataram period is affirmed by the *Serat Rama*. A king who gave way to unbridled harshness and anger, because of anxiety to be feared and obeyed, was also condemned. Such a king was likened to a goat that attacked any piece of wood held up before him.[221]

Such behavior, of course, revealed an uncontrolled emotion, which for the Javanese was a highly unbecoming trait,

In a society, where the belief in fate was so strong, reaction against an oppressive rule lay in evasion rather than in interference. At a time when population was sparse, untilled land was available in abundance, and especially when wooded areas and mountain ranges could still provide hiding places, such tactics were most feasible. This custom seems to be quite old, for the *Nitisastra*, a translation of the Old-Javanese *Niticastra* dating from the end of Madjapahit (about fifteenth century), states that a king who

did not keep an eye [on his subjects] and had a cruel disposition will be left and evaded by his subjects.[222]

The *Bajan Budiman*, a Javanese book of Persian origin,[223] also contains a passage, which tells us of such evasion of oppression. The vizier, Suleksan, at his wit's end because he could no longer provide the monarch of Ngesam

---

219 Jasadipura I, *op. cit.*, p. 238.

220 Schrieke, *op. cit.*, Book One, III, 6, pp. 88 - 95.

221 Jasadipura I, *op. cit.*, p. 38.

222 *Niticastra*, point 27.

223 This book has the well-known frame-story of the king who married a maiden every day only to put her to death the following morning, and who was cured of this cruel habit by the daughter of his vizier who told him a long chain of stories night after night.

with a girl every night, informed the king that

> the wealthy and the small people alike have fled into the mountains,
> the town is depopulated; how ever can one possibly find a girl?[224]

A more recent and historically dependable example comes from a narrative of the journey of Governor General van Imhoff (1743-1750) in 1744. When speaking of the river Tangerang as the partition between V.O.C.- and Banten-territory, the narrative relates that many people from the Company's side of the river were migrating to the other side because it was said that there buying one's freedom from statute-labor was less expensive.[225] A report from a former administrator of the V.O.C. about the Surabaja region, dated December 31, 1812, suggested that the amount of forced deliveries be reduced in order to prevent a "lessening of the population."[226] People fled from difficult conditions during the first half of the 1930's when, because of the Great Depression, it was very difficult to earn enough money in the villages to pay the comparatively low land-rent; many farmers gave up their already small shares of the village communal-land in order to be freed from paying taxes. In a country where peoples' living is almost exclusively based on the produce of the soil, abandoning that soil indicates a really desperate situation.[227] But we may presume that during the earlier period, especially when forced by war, such disappearances into the mountains were temporary; the peasants would return to their villages when the dangers had passed. Under a truly oppressive rule (usually when the tax burden was overwhelming), the people would seek permanent refuge in other countries or at least in more remote areas of their own country beyond the reach of the king's men.

---

224 Ch. Hooykaas, *Tantri, de Middel-Javaansche Pancatantra-bewerking*, Leiden, 1929, Appendix V.

225 "Reis van den G. G. G. W. Baron van Imhoff in en door de Jakatrasche-Bovenlanden 1744," *Bijdragen*, New Series, Vol. VII, 1864, p. 230.

226 F. J. Rothenbuhler, "Rapport van den Staat en Gesteldheid van het Landschap Sourabaija," *VBG*, Vol. XLI, 1881, p. 37.

227 Therefore in times of war the population was pictured as being in a state of *wajang-wujungan* (going hither and thither without purpose),and the *Babad Tanah Djawi* says "the people did not have the opportunity to till the soil, constantly moving to and fro." (*Babad Tanah Djawi*, p. 245).

Van Vollenhoven mentioned two kinds of collective protest by the people. One was the right of villages to place themselves under the jurisdiction of another administrator or certain members of a ruling family group or another tax collector. The second one was the right to complain to a higher official in a procession called *nggogol*.[228] This means of showing public sentiment in a procession seems to be quite old. Criminals caught, thieves and rebels also were brought to the authorities in procession,and the preventive meaning of such a public showing is obvious.

Another public show of concern was the custom of doing *pepe* (to sit in the full rays of the sun) in the great square of the *Kraton* in view of the king's audience hall (*sitinggil*) until the king agreed to hear the petition. Such an act contained the implication that the petitioner laid his life in his Lord's hand. *Pepe* might also indicate a petition for clemency.[229]

In connection with demonstrations of the public's contempt, we must examine another weathervane of public opinion in Javanese society, folk-humor, expressed in the jokes of the clown-figures of Javanese plays, first of all, in the *wajang kulit* but also and more importantly in other folkshows The most common are — at least for the later period — the *wajang wong* (*wajang* plays staged by actors, not puppets), the *ketoprak* (a kind of operetta), and, in East Java, the *ludruk*. Such expressions of public opinion were never re-corded because they did not belong to the court-sphere. In Javanese society, clowns and jesters traditionally have had a certain immunity from punishment for their witty and sometimes stinging remarks about current situations or persons of importance. Dr. Pigeaud, as we have seen above,[230] explains their immunity by pointing out that actors were thought "dangerous" in the sense of being magically powerful. Perhaps actors were thought to be magically powerful because they impersonated ancestors and other famous people of the past and thus "actually" contained their spirits; in the case of clowns, their abnormal behavior "actually" gave them superhuman powers. Perhaps, as Pigeaud thinks, their ability to release human emotions and passions

---

228 C. van Vollenhoven, *Javaansch Adatrecht*, Leiden, 1923, p. 42.
229 *Babad Tanah Djawi*, pp. 133, 148. Also Oudemans, *op. cit.*, p. 199. The act of *pepe* is here regulated in the Pramatan Patuh, codified in 1869: "Doing *pepe* without valid reason is made susceptible to punishment."
230 Page 67.

made them "dangerous." These are questions which will make a further study of this subject highly interesting. The *garebeg*-processions of the kings of Jogjakarta and Surakarta[231] were of entirely solemn and dignified character but, strikingly, two figures, the *tjantang balungs*, who were the *lurahs* (chiefs) of the dancing girls in the city, marched along in the procession,[232] in strangely foolish attire and acting jocularly all the time. One might assume that the magical aspect of their theatrical profession made their participation in the grave occasion appropriate. During the Japanese occupation (1942-1945), a rule of torture and cruelty, perhaps unconsciously relying on the old immunity, a *badut* (clown) of a well-known *ludruk*-group, Tjak Durasim of Surabaja, frankly and openly criticized, or better, made fun of the abject conditions of the people. Unfortunately for him, the Japanese military government did not recognize his customary immunity. The *dalang*, by way of the *panakawans* (clown puppets), assumes the same privilege of commenting and criticizing.

Folk-opinion is expressed in yet another way. Short phrases, rhymes or pithy words were composed, especially in the Surakarta region, and became so popular that they were known to virtually everybody, becoming a kind of a street-song shouted back and forth between groups of strolling young people or sung by children at play. Such "limericks," sometimes not very clear in meaning, dealt with what was of current interest to the common man. They might be of a very innocent character like the rhyme which expressed surprise at the ability of motor cars to go their way without horse or cow in front. A street-song from the beginning of this century went:

tit tuwit damar mati ungalna
kintel lungguh dingklik sabuk nekel ora duwe duwit

tit tuwit (the sound of a whistle) the lamps went out
    so turn them up.
a frog sitting on a stool, a waistband clasp of nickel
    but no money.

---

231 *Garebeg* processions from the palace to the mosque, Masdjid Ageng, were held on certain holy days.
232 I. Groneman, *De Garebeg's te Ngajogjakarta*, 's-Gravenhage, 1895, p. 33.

Another version which read *"muliha"* (go home) instead of *"ungalna"* at the end of the first line made people think it was a kind of prophecy of World War II, the sounds of whistles referring to the sirens of the air-raid warning system; the second line ridicules the many penniless dandies of the time. Sometimes the "limericks" tersely condemned conditions and situations which were thought improper. During the Revolutionary years after the proclamation of Indonesian independence in 1945, a street-song appeared which ridiculed the incompetence of hastily appointed leaders and authorities. One can assume that this way of giving vent to the public's dissatisfaction could be encountered too in earlier times although, lacking records, we are restricted to examples from the very near past. What effect street-songs have had on the reigning monarch is difficult to evaluate now, but a wise ruler would most certainly not disregard any signs of discontent which might be manipulated by a would-be usurper.

To express rebellion against a lawful master, the Javanese used the words *mbalik* (lit.: to turn around and stand face to face), *mbeka* (to be recalcitrant), *mbalela* (to revolt), and the phrase *madeg kraman*[233] which can be translated as "to set up one's own government," obviously with the purpose of establishing a new and independent territorial power or even a new government challenging an existing one. Indeed if we examine the revolts and rebellions during the Mataram period and even as late as the nineteenth century, the purpose of an uprising seemed almost always to set up an independent government, complete with all ceremonial paraphernalia and a full set of dignitaries. This was even true of the most insignificant disturbances, for the idea of magical identification made such imitation essential to the success of the undertaking. Raden Surjakusuma, a son of Pangeran Puger, rebelled at the beginning of Sunan Amangkurat III's reign (1703-1708). He fashioned (*ngreka*) a palace complete with *alun-alun* at the village Ngenta-enta,[234] a place which a later rebel, Ki Mas Dana (the *Babad Tanah Djawi* gives the year 1711 for Dana's rebellion) also used as a base for his operations. The latter also was said to have "already appointed *mantris* and *bupatis* (officials)"[235] to implement his "state." A rebellion against the Dutch colonial government around 1880

---

233 *Madeg*: to become, to make oneself; *ngraman*: to set up a new settlement.
234 The word "ngenta" means: to simulate, to copy an original.
235 *Babad Tanah Djawi*, p. 305.

was not very serious because of its utterly naive, traditional planning: a certain Malangjuda of Purbalingga in Central Java, intending to become the supreme lord of Java with the title *wali*, appointed three kings, one for the West, one for the Middle, and one for East Java. In anticipation of his coming success he had already secured four *kuluk kanigara* (a brimless, black headgear, ornamented with strips of gold), the ceremonial headgear of Javanese dignitaries of high rank[236] to be worn at the official inauguration. The adventure ended dismally. In the disturbances at Klaten around the 1880's, the rebels had formed a government complete with all the high officials, royal decrees and royal seals.[237]

A magical and religious orientation is evident from the fact that many usurpers began their efforts by avoiding or leaving the capital, that is, the *kraton*, to live in seclusion and meditation, hoping to strengthen themselves inwardly for the coming confrontation of force. An early example, although under circumstances which were slightly different, was King Airlanggawho, after the collapse of King Dharmavamsa Anantavikrama's rule (991-1017), hid himself for two years and lived as an ascetic in a monastery in the forests of Panaraga, wearing treebark-clothes[238] in order to prepare himself for the struggle to recapture his father-in-law's throne. The *Babad Tanah Djawi* mentions Raden Punta, a nephew of Amangkurat II (1677-1703), who

> *ndedagan* (meditated at the foot of a grave) in the burial grounds of Tegal Arum, with the intention to revolt.[239]

The hiding place of the famous rebel Untung Surapati in the mountains of Ngantang of East Java (which contain caves) was most probably a place of meditation. So was the cave of Selarong in Jogjakarta, where Prince Dipanegara, the great leader of the Java War of 1825-1830, spent days of seclusion in preparation for the war. The felt need for inner strength and unquestionably also for magical powers (especially invulnerability) made it natural that in the late nineteenth and twentieth centuries the initiative

236 Drewes, *op. cit.*, p. 31.
237 I. Groneman, *Uit en Over Midden Java*, Zutphen, 1391, p. 70.
238 J. G. de Casparis, *Airlangga*, Inaugural speech, Surabaja, 1958.
239 *Babad Tanah Djawi*, p. 259.

to revolt should most often be in the hands of *gurus* and *kyais*, men who by virtue of their religious life had already acquired the reputation for possessing supernatural or at least more than human capacities. The authority of rebel *kyais* and *gurus* presumably owed more to these assumed magical powers than to their religious piety. Moreover, the *kyais* could easily translate general discontent against a foreign rule into the Islamic *djihad* (Jav.: *perang sabil*, the war against the *kapir*, the unbeliever); participation in the rebellion thus became the duty of a true Moslem. Such was the case with the serious uprisings in Tjilegon, Banten (July 1888) and in Klaten (in about 1880), and with the rather insignificant rebellion of the *guru* (teacher of religious learning) Imam Sempurna[240] in another Surakarta district (1888) who, together with his small group of followers (*murid*,disciples) among whom were several women, fought futilely to his death. And of course Pangeran Dipanegara's main advisor and fellow commander, Kyai Madja, served both as an inspiring source of supernatural powers as well as an influential leader of the Moslem community. The white robes the rebels wore[241] and the blind fanaticism with which they fought revealed their confidence that their leader's magic powers made them invulnerable to the sharpness of steel and even to the penetrating power of bullets or shells. Such beliefs in invulnerability still found acceptance during the Indonesian Revolution. Myth-making was always an important element in war and accounted for the leader-commander's very crucial role.

Another characteristic of Javanese uprisings was the seeming preference for certain places to begin a rebellion or to use as a stronghold. Professor Schrieke[242] cites Kediri in East Java as an example of such a favored region. The Alas Ketangga (the forests of Ketangga), mentioned in the *Serat Djaja Baja* as the abode of the coming *ratu adil* (The Just King), is located in Kediri. The *Babad Tanah Djawi* mentions the village Ngenta-enta twice as a center of rebellion.[243] The failure of previous rebellions did not seem to discourage later pretenders from choosing the same headquarters, a fact that might be explained by the unshakable

---

240 I. Groneman, *Uit en Over Midden Java*, p. 27.
241 Drewes, *op. cit.*, p. 33. Also *Babad Tanah Djawi*, p. 315.
242 Schrieke, *op. cit.*, p. 94. *Babad Tanah Djawi*, p. 338.
243 *Babad Tanah Djawi*, pp. 262, 306.

belief in fate which ordained that these places be the starting places of a new and better state.

Leaders of rebellions were of diverse origins. Quite a few were princes or regional authorities, e.g., adipati Pragola of Pati,[244] Tumenggung Djaja Puspita of Surabaja,[245] and Trunadjaja of Madura. There were also men of the common people, e.g., the Tjilegon rebel leader of the Klaten uprising mentioned above, but it is apparent that the commoner's goal was no different than that of a rebel prince; it was to become the traditional and conservative king, the inevitable and predestined leader of the community.

The belief that the coming of the *ratu adil* (The Just King) is inevitable developed from the Indian belief in the four world-periods (*yuga*) going in cycle from good (Krta-) declining via Treta and Dvapara Yuga to evil (Kali-Yuga). The Islamic belief in a coming messiah, the Imam Mahdi, also contributed to the Javanese belief in the forthcoming emergence of a righteous and just king after a period of upheaval and moral decline.[246] In Javanese such a period was called the *djaman kalabendu* (period of Kala and Anger). The Javanese associate the world *Kala* with mishap and destruction, the characteristics of the Indian deity Kala or Mahakala the demoniac aspect of god çiwa, who represents death and time, the two powers of destruction. The name "Herutjakra," a combination of *heru* of Arabic origin (Arab. *chair*: good, fortune) and *tjakra* of Indian origin (Skrt. *cakra*: disc, wheel),[247] was given as the name of the coming king. Two rebel princes had assumed this title, both named Pangeran Dipanegara; the first, during the reign of Paku Buwana I (1703-1719), with Bupati Djaja Puspita of Surabaja rebelled against his own father, and the second led the Java War of 1825-1830. Dr. Drewes, in his dissertation, studied the problem of the *ratu-adil* movement extensively.[248]

Politically, the convenience of the *ratu adil* concept is obvious; it justified usurpation. As for the time of decline which had to precede the

---

244 *Ibid.*, p. 110.
245 *Ibid.*, p. 307.
246 As we have seen (pp. 40, 44 above), eschatological speculations form the main theme of the *Serat Djaja Baja*.
247 *Herutjakra* reminds us of *njakrawati*, the world ruler.
248 Drewes, *op. cit.*, especially Ch. III, pp. 129-193. See also Th. W. Juynboll, *Handleiding tot de kennis van de Mohammedaansche Wet*, Leiden, 1930, p. 338.

emergence of a *ratu adil*, there were always scores of reasons to be found with which one could rationalize one's discontent. A student, however, might measure the intensity of discontent during a certain period by the frequency with which such *ratu-adil* movements appeared, and the breadth of discontent by the number of followers gathered or the size of territory affected. Whether strict personal motives or a general discontent formed the incentive towards a rebellion can also be estimated. So in judging rebellions in older Javanese history one must not stare blindly at the apparent and traditional goal of every uprising, namely the acquisition of the throne for the leader of the revolt, but one should take into consideration also the cosmological principles and beliefs which explained the inevitability of the king's downfall.

CHAPTER THREE
THE TECHNICAL IMPLEMENTATION OF KINGSHIP: THE PROBLEM OF ADMINISTRATION

Objectives and Tools of Administration

The Idea of Self-sufficiency in Government

With the all-dominating position of the king in state-life, administration as the technical tool of kingship had to reflect the king's major concern, the preservation of Harmony. This need, which was expressed as *ndjaga tata-tentreming pradja* (to guard the order and tranquillity of the state), determined the *pangreh-pradja's* (or *paprentahan*: administration) major and most important task, namely maintaining security. In practice this meant guarding against any possible disturbance from an outside foe as well as any internal crime or irregularity which might disturb the balance between the two cosmic spheres. Protecting and encouraging religious observance was a vital means of retaining such a balance, and therefore had to be included as an objective of the administration. The *Serat Rama* attributes the task of destroying the outside enemy to the god Brama, and wiping out internal crime to god Jama.[1] It also stresses the necessity of eliminating crimes endangering religious practice, so that those who "did ascetic practice and worship" would then be able to pursue their task for the blessed welfare of the realm.[2] Protection and encouragement of religious life from olden times

---

1 See page 43.
2 Jasadipura I, op. cit., p. 41.

on took the form of granting special rights to religious groups and communities. Usually gifts of land were distributed by the king to religious communities, not merely as a means of subsistence, but primarily so that they would be financially strong enough to perform their religious services satisfactorily for the welfare of the king and so of his realm. These domains in the Old-Javanese period were called *dharmas* or *dharma lepas* (freeholds).[3] In the Later Mataram period there were several kinds of *desa perdikan* (free villages), many of which were to be found in the region of old Bagelen and Panaraga (Madiun). The importance of the religious element in Later Mataram state life was also reflected in the existence of a separate and seemingly more independent administrative department, the *Reh Pangulon* (Office of the Head of the Clergy), which responsible for matters of religion including rendering justice in disputes under the jurisdiction of the Islamic laws. This department, however, as an incorporated part of the state administration[4] with a state-wide jurisdiction, did not seem to be very old; at least there are no indications that may justify such a conclusion. In fact, the non-existence in Islam of a widely organized, hierarchical clergy in the Christian sense does not support such a view. The institution of the *pengulu* possibly was older, for he was the head of the clergy in the main mosque in the king's capital and only gradually was he incorporated into the administrative system as head of a special division. Dr. Juynboll, writing about the Mangkunegaran principality in 1882, reports that the *pengulu* at court had his say about the appointment of the lower *pengulu naibs* who each administered the religious affairs of a certain number of villages.[5] These lower officials were not thought of as belonging to the king's administration for, unlike the other royal officials, they did not receive either income or token appanage from the king; from early times on, they had to make their living from the regular *djakat* and *pitrah* levies, the obligatory contributions which Islam prescribed to its followers. The levy was in the form of a certain portion of every *gedeng* (a kind of measurement) of ears of rice. The

---

3 Pigeaud, *Java in the 14th Century*, Vol. IV, pp. 223, 226.

4 In 1935, in Surakarta, strangely enough this department was called *Kawedanan Yogaswara*, the last name having an entirely Hinduistic notion.

5 A. W. T. Juynboll, "*Kleine bijdragen* over den Islam op Java," Bijdragen, 4th series, Vol. VI, 1882 (30), p. 281. See also: Rouffaer, *op. cit.*, p. 61.

officials also received gifts or contributions in the course of performing marriages, dividing inheritances and the like. In 1881, this was also true for the regency of Surabaja, at that time no longer a part of the Mataram kingdom.[6]

The existence of bands of bandits and robbers seems to have formed an established and quite ancient institution, not only in Javanese society, but everywhere in the world at one time or other.[7] Dacoity in India and Burma, the existence of secret societies in China, and the pirate colonies along the Straits of Malacca and the Sulu Islands of the Philippines attest to the persistence of these institutions in history. Piracy may even have been a means of creating nuclei of political power out of which strong states might be built.[8] The *Serat Rama* is quite explicit that criminals had to be disposed of without delay, just as one would dispose of caterpillars,[9] and taking the law into one's own hands against a criminal was not considered a crime. The existence or nonexistence of such bands of robbers always formed a standard to measure the efficiency and stability of a regime. Bandits threw the realm into a state of *resah* (Kr., *rusuh* Ng.: unstable, unsafe) when the king's rule was weak, for they would lay low and seek refuge in the woods under a reign of strength and ability.[10] When hiding in remote and secluded areas they might even form regular village organizations with fellow-villains and their families. Such a village of brigands is mentioned in the encyclopaedic *Serat Tjentini*, a work written in the 1820's, in which the powerful brigand leader is called the village *petinggi* (village headman) and it was he

who controlled the roads through the forests and mountain range.[11]

It was not unusual, even in the first decades of the twentieth century, that,

6 Rothenbuhler, *op. cit.*, p. 21.
7 D. H. Meyer, "Over het bendewezen op Java," *Indonesië*, III, July 1949-May 1950, p. 179.
8 Nicholas Tarling, *Piracy and Politics in the Malay World*, Melbourne, 1963, p. 4. See also p. 10.
9 Jasadipura I, *op. cit.*, p. 43.
10 *Ibid.*, p. 36.
11 *Serat Tjentini*, ed. Bataviaasch Genootschap van Kunsten en Wetenschappen, Batavia, 1912-1915, Vol. VII -VIII, p. 112ff.

when a certain region riddled by brigandage and robbery was pacified, a local "converted" — usually only half-converted — leader of a band was made a village headman and burdened with the duty to govern and appease his region. Such a policy was based on one of the basic principles of administration in Java: choose officials with regional responsibility primarily on the basis of the influence he already has in the community. It was said and it was believed that incorporating such robber-chiefs made *their* particular region free from the disturbances of robbery and brigandage.

When brigands had *de facto* power over certain areas, they imposed a kind of forced tribute on the villagers and traders passing through.[12] Physical force, the bands' sole tool to enforce their authority, was used to make them, if only temporarily, the masters in areas where the king's authority was ineffective. The bandits' pillage or looting might be seen in terms of the accepted right to ransack a defeated adversary's *kraton* or *dalem* (manor) for riches and women (*ndjarah lan mbebojong* or *mbebandang*).[13] Javanese stories tell about kings (for instance Ken Angrok) and saints (Sunan Kalidjaga) who had been robbers,but the stories stress the unusualness of this background for a great man. If we consider all these aspects of brigandage together, we notice the apparent similarity between the rule of brigand bands and that of the kings of the past. First, brigand bands, living an independent perilous existence within the state, assumed the royal practices of levy and pillage-in-war in the territories they controlled. Secondly, like the brigands, the monarchical state in Old Java, however intricate and elaborate its organization and structure might be, relied primarily on the use of physical force to establish its authority.

Taxation, in a sense, is tribute in exchange for the lord's protection. Thus we can understand why taxation and the collection of taxes, in the form of money, produce, and labor, formed the third important task of the state. It is interesting to observe here that taxation was not mentioned or discussed in the many *piwulangs* we have used for this study although

---

12 Meyer describes brigandage in Banten in very recent times; tribute, there, was called *wang ngaraksa* (Sundanese: safeguard-money). It is striking that watchmen-organiza-tions elsewhere in Java in the revolution of 1945-50, at least some of them, were thought of as organizations of former brigands. This corresponds entirely with Meyer's description. Meyer, *op. cit.*, p. 187. See also *Pigeaud*, Java in the 14th Century, Vol. IV, p. 476.

13 *Babad Tanah Djawi*, pp. 112, 126, 131, 135.

it did form an essential and finely regulated part of state life. It was not deemed necessary to discuss the moral justification of taxes and perhaps as a material matter they were not worthy of deep consideration.[14]

Taxation is dealt with in the *Serat Rama*; however it treated not the principles of taxation but only the ideal characteristics of a tax collector.

> if you want to get tribute-money, you have to choose another official, namely one who has the character of a goat…the habit of one with the character of a goat is not being used to cleanliness …he must be untiring in insistence and only stop when he has achieved his ends, never looking to the right nor to the left, urgent in his persistence.[15]

Maintenance of justice was another major concern of the king in preserving Harmony. The older term *mbebeneri* for rendering justice has now fallen more and more into disuse and has been replaced by the Arabic derived term *ngadili* ['adl (Arab.): justice], which has the literal meaning of "making right." The newer term is perfectly in accord with the idea of setting straight the balance of tranquillity, the sense in which "harmony" is understood by the Javanese in the context of macro- and micro-cosmos relationship.

Winter discusses a characteristic of Javanese law in his description of the judicature in the kingdom of Surakarta at about the middle of the nineteenth century, namely conciliation, or compromise, whereby the king's official, the territorial administrator,[16] was required to attempt to settle a case with an agreement between the parties concerned. Winter wrote that such a method of solution could be applied to "all cases, of any kind whatsoever," thus including civil as well as criminal cases, in European legal terminology. In the summation of the duties of the Tumenggung-redi or the Kliwon-redi — the *redi* denoting that those officials were in charge of police supervision — the task of trying for a peaceful solution

14 See further Appendix II.
15 Jasadipura I, *op. cit.*, p. 40.
16 C. F. Winter, "Regtspleging over de onderdanen van Z. H. den Soesoehoenan van Soerakarta," *Tijdschrift voor Neërlandsch Indië, Batavia*, 1844, p. 123.

is mentioned as one of the important duties.[17] Actually, if we look up an older lawbook from Bali, which was taken by Dr. Jonkers as a subject for his dissertation, we can find that criminal acts were treated as matters of civil law. Article 45 of the lawbook for instance says that stealing of the fruits of the land is punishable by death if done at night, but if it is done in the daytime it can be nullified by a compensation of thrice the value of the stolen goods, which would come to the benefit of the plaintiff. Article 24 tells of a compensation of two times the value of the stolen wares plus a ransom and a fine of respectively "8000" and "4000" which came to the king if the thief should plead for preservation of his life,[18] From this fragment of Balinese law written in Old-Javanese, in conjunction with others, Jonker concluded that "indigenous law throughout the whole Archipelago" had a civil law character,[19] tending to consider all cases of litigation as affecting only the parties concerned. An agreement between the parties themselves would then eliminate the cause of the disturbance and thereby restore the tranquillity of both cosmic spheres.

But, perhaps from the point of view of practicality in state policy, the reason for the tendency to grant parties the right to solve disputes independent of outside interference, even from the state, must be sought more in a characteristic typical of state administration in Old Java, and, as further study will undoubtedly show, of feudal administration in general. That is, the effort to avoid the problems inherent in intricate and complex organization by keeping state administration as simple as possible. This was accomplished by creating a system of highly autonomous and usually also financially self-sufficient administrative units, be they territorial like a district or a regency, or functional like the department of religious affairs and the department of the Kalangs (woodcutters and woodworkers). Probably the Javanese did not intentionally differentiate between territorial and functional units and we do so only for the sake of convenience. According to Rouffaer,[20] before 1831, there were seven

---

17 *Ibid.*, p. 23.
18 J. C. G. Jonker, *Een Oud-Javaansch Wetboek*, dissertation, Leiden, 1885, p. 101. Jonker says the code is "relatively old."
19 *Ibid.*, p. 22.
20 Rouffaer, *op. cit.*, p. 60. See also *Babad Tanah Djawi*, p. 16. 1831 was the year of the reorganization of the Kasunanan (Surakarta) and Kasultanan (Jogjakarta) territory in response to the last great reduction of these kingdoms in 1830 after the Java war when they assumed their present sizes.

ranks of officials lower than *Wedana* and *Kliwon* (these two being regarded as belonging to the higher officials) namely, from highest to lowest: the *Panewu*; *Penatus* (or Mantri); *Paneket*; *Panalawe* or *Panglawe*; *Panigangdjung*; *Panandjung*; and *Panakikil*. The names indicate that they had respectively 1000, 100, 50, 25, 4 and 2 *tjatjah*[21] under their authority. This seemed to indicate that in former times the rank of an official was always measured according to the *tjatjah* (count, thus the number of men) under his jurisdiction. In this system of administrative units, in accord with the character of simplicity of organization, the leader was given the sole, undivided responsibility and undivided power within the boundaries of his function, necessary to accomplishing his all-inclusive task: *ndjaga tatatentreming pradja* (to guard the tranquillity of the realm) mentioned above. That the officials' full responsibility had to be counterbalanced by the king's absolute confidence in them was put forth again and again in the *Serat Rama*, even with regard to a subdued enemy re-installed as the king's vassal.[22] Since he possessed full power and thus full responsibility, the official could expect harsh punishment, including death, if he failed to execute his duty to the satisfaction of his lord. The *Babad Tanah Djawi* includes the classic case of the two commanders who led the Mataram troops in 1628 in the attack on Batavia, capital of the merchant empire of the United East-India Company of the Dutch (V.O.C.). Rice-stores were set up along the route of the troops and a general levy putting the entire Mataram forces into battle was drawn from all dependencies from the Priangan highlands of West Java to Sampang on the island of Madura. All this testifies to the great importance which Sultan Agung (1613-1645) attached to the undertaking, and thus also to the great personal responsibility of its commanders. Punishment with death for failure[23] was in this case quite acceptable to the Javanese. The *bupati* (regional chief) of Pasuruhan in East Java, who fled to Kartasura when Raden Tirtakusuma of Winongan rebelled within his territory of jurisdiction, was sentenced to be put to death by kris because

his crime being that he failed in taking care of the province of

---

21 For the meaning of *tjatjah* see Appendix II.
22 Jasadipura I, *op. cit.*, pp. 38, 39, 44, 448.
23 *Babad Tanah Djawi*, p. 139.

Pasuruhan [because] he would not meet the Winongan troops in battle.[24]

Such a responsibility was also stressed in Mangkunegara IV's writing.[25] The king's officials, from high to low, were held accountable not only in matters of great importance, but also in their daily tasks. This was evident from the many cases where the official in charge had to pay a fine for irregularities occurring in his district; mostly these cases had to do with crimes, like serious injury or murder, for which the culprit could not be identified or could not be arrested.[26]

The state also followed a policy of allowing the *desa* (village) a certain degree of autonomous self-sufficiency especially in the field of security. The policy was implemented by instituting collective responsibility for some crimes and other illegal acts; thus not only were the inhabitants of the premises where the crime or deed was committed responsible, but also the neighbors who lived *madjupat* (on all four sides) within a certain number of *tjengkal* (7.95 feet for each *tjengkal*) from the scene of the crime.[27] In some criminal cases, the whole *desa* and even its *mantjapat* and *mantjalima*,[28] the contiguous villages and the *desas* next to them,[29] were held responsible. Such was the case with the crime of robbery with manslaughter, in which the delinquents could be neither caught nor identified. In fact, as a general rule the villagers were collectively held responsible for the security of their *desa*, not only to the benefit of themselves, but also to that of strangers, peddlers and traders, and especially to that of royal officials who had to stay overnight in the *desa* in the execution of their duties.[30] Even the markets, which were let out by the king to Chinese entrepreneurs, had to be guarded by the villagers.[31]

Self-sufficiency seemed to be the main principle in state financing too.

---

24 *Ibid.*, p. 307.
25 Mangkunegara IV, *op. cit.*, p. 67.
26 Law "Angger Ageng," art. 4, 10; also art. 7, 22. Law "Angger Arubiru," art. 14 (Oudemans, op. cit., Vol. II, pp. 54, 82; 74, 102; 13).
27 Law "Angger Pradata Akir," art. 8 (Oudemans, op. cit., Vol. II, p. 28); Law "Surja Alam" (Soeripto, *Ontwik-kelingsgang der Vorstenlandsche Wetboeken*, Dissertation, Leiden, 1929, p. 218.
28 Rouffaer, *op. cit.*, p. 57.
29 Winter, "Regtspleging," p. 124. Law "Angger Ageng," art. 4.
30 Law "Angger Ageng," art. 3.
31 *Ibid.*, art. 23.

The finance system of Later Mataram can be called "salary-financing," for out of the salary which the official earned (entirely in the form of appanages called *lungguh*) he was expected to pay all the expenses entailed in the performance of his tasks and duties.[32] The official could defray the expenses of his work because the full authority given to him by the king enabled him to exact contributions and levy of labor from his district. But since he was required to be self-sufficient he had no recourse to financial sources other than those prescribed.[33] Several articles of the law "Angger Gunung" codified in 1846, and so of a rather recent date, have to do with this principle of self-financing. Articles 4-14 which regulated the different "postal stations" on the stagecoach service put the burden of providing relief-bearers or relief-horseteams (*tundan*) entirely on the official concerned. Articles 22 and 23 ordered the responsible officials to arrange all that was necessary for the reception of the king or of "great Dutch dignitaries" (*tuwan-tuwan* gede) while they were at rest stations.[34] This meant that the officials had to provide refreshment or even food and entertainment; at least a *gamelan*-orchestra had to play upon the arrival of the guests. However, for this purpose, at least some officials were given special additional appanages. The burdens of providing a worthy reception to passing dignitaries moved an official to comment to *patih* Pringgalaja:

> You could not possibly bear these burdens, for your *sawahs* (rice-fields) would all be gone.

He would have to rent out all his appanages to finance these expenditures.[35]

The "Angger Gunung" also confirms our conclusion about self-sufficient financing in a negative way. This law creates a new administrative office which financed the maintenance of the "postal station" buildings and also of roads and the bridges on, presumably, only the main roads. This office was called *kantor* from the Dutch "kantoor" (office) which

---

32 See also: H. J. van Mook, "Kuta Gede," in *The Indonesian Town*, The Hague, 1958, p. 302.
33 See further: Appendix II.
34 Oudemans, *op. cit.*, Vol. II, pp. 200, 201.
35 *Babad Mataram*, Vol. V, p. 114.

indicates that it had not existed earlier. It is not certain whether this office was that of the Dutch Resident as representative of the Netherland-Indies Government, which is very likely, or a part of the king's administration proper. Nevertheless it is clear that the system of central financing prescribed was new to the Javanese.

It is well known that the peasant soldiers had to provide their own food and lodging (the latter only in the form of a sleeping mat: *klasa*) on expeditions.[36] This fact also is an example of the policy of requiring self-sufficiency.

The rule of autonomous financing for all parts of the administration suits exceedingly well a state governed by the ideal of non-interference. Non-interference also was quite in accord with the self-sufficiency of the agrarian life in the Javanese *desa*, whose narrow *espace social* required neither differentiation of occupation nor intensive communication with the outside world. Letting life take its course, in accord with conservative traditionalism, the state became the guardian against disturbance, interfering only when there was a threat to tranquillity. The word *pangajoman* (giving shelter from rain and sun, from *ajom*: shaded) along with the *waringin* (ficus benghalensis), the giant banyan tree with its dense and widespread foliage, became the symbol of kingly rule. Inside the realms, tranquillity and regularity was the state's main aim, *not* active stimulation towards progress.

The full and undivided authority of the *punggawa* (official) and the autonomous self-sufficiency of his position made him a man of broad responsibilities, and this was especially so if he had territorial responsibility. It is therefore not surprising that, within his region, he wielded the powers of administrator, judge and commander of the local contingent of troops.[37] The elaborate household of the king and the multiplicity of royal duties (international relations, the army, ceremonies, etc.) demanded a division of functions with the king in the controlling position. The fact that regional officials held undivided power made it

---

36 Schrieke, *op. cit.*, Vol. II, Book 2, 2, especially p. 128.

37 Dr. Soeripto also hinted that the king's officials were administrators and judges at once, which seemed to be an old Indonesian monoduality. (Soeripto, *op. cit.*, p. 175). The *najakas*, heads of the departments of administration at court, were all members of the Balemangu-court under the chairmanship of the Raden Adipati (title of the Grand Vizier) (Winter, "Regtspleging," p. 100. See also: Rushton Coulborn, *Feudalism in History*, Princeton, 1956, p. 5).

essential that they be chosen with great care. As we have seen,[38] selection of officials was considered a crucial and difficult royal task because high morals, a deep Sense of duty and great courage were required for such all-embracing work.

Just as for the king, a regional official's main problem was how to accumulate sufficient influence in his region to make his task agreeable. His authority to a certain extent of course depended on the fact that his was an aspect of the king's (and thus also of God's) supreme right to rule. State administration in Later Mataram was imitative in its perception of power and authority, and in its ideological aspect. We will observe later that this was also the case in its technical-administrative aspect. Regional administration was, from top to bottom, entirely repetitive, but of course within consecutively smaller territories.

The Prijaji

The positions and functions in the king's administration were filled by *punggawas* (officials), also called by the more general term *abdidalem* (the king's servants). Throughout the centuries these officials, from the highest to the lowest, had gradually become a social class with an exclusive set of beliefs and values; they formed the social stratum between the king and the small group of princes of royal blood (*para bendara*) and the great mass of private citizens who, irrespective of wealth or means of living, were called the *tijang alit* in *Krama* or the *wong tjilik* (the small people) in Ngoko.[39] In the older Javanese society, the ruling elite was thus composed of two groups, the aristocracy of blood (the king and the *para bendara*) and the aristocracy by profession who were called *kawula*, the name used for the king's subjects in general. As the *Babad Tanah Djawi* indicates, officials were also called *bala* (subjects,

---

38 See p. 50.

39 *Krama* or "high"-Javanese and *Ngoko* or "low"-Javanese are the two basic social dialects in the Javanese language, with some other intermediate forms. These dialects were how ever not spoken only within, but to a greater extent between the social strata of Javanese society to indicate degrees of respect and intimacy of relation between the speakers. It forms a linguistic etiquette of a rather intricate pattern. Dr. Clifford Geertz has reserved to this subject a short but not an undeserving paragraph in his book, although the location of his study is hardly proper to study the delicate intricacies of etiquette in the Javanese language. (Clifford Geertz, *The Religion of Java*, Glencoe, I11., 1960, pp. 248-260.)

troops)[40] although since they were in the service of the monarch they might occupy the same functional position. Thus, Javanese society of the Later Mataram period had an elite group which a commoner might enter, but only by becoming a servant of the king, an official. The word *kulawisuda* or *kawulawisuda*, which Gericke's dictionary translates as "raised to a higher rank" and which is a combination of the words *kawula* (subject, servant) and *wisuda* (to promote),[41] implies the possibility of entering the elite and also that such entrance was effected only via the road of officialdom. Another phrase denoting promotion to high rank is *sinengkakaken ingaluhur* which has the connotation that the person has gained favor with the king and has joined the *para luhur* (the high), the top-elite of the ruling aristocracy.

The official's relationship to the monarch was unconditional and submissive for only the king could grant *kamukten* (welfare and prosperity);[42] this had to be true in an agrarian-based state when the king had the absolute right of disposal over the land, and officials were paid with the usufruct of land in the form of *lungguh* (appanages). This was also stated clearly in Paku Buwana's IX writing,[43] and the *Wulangreh* expresses it as follows:

> there is nothing to be compared to serving the king; he will see the king's court-yard and will be respected and have a name [in society], and then there is also the appanage ; ...serving can be likened to debris drifting in the ocean, going wherever it is commanded to.[44]

Unconditional submission is also required of the armed forces. The troops are the arrows of the bowman; the commander (*senapati*)[45] aims them according to his will.

Although Javanese society had an open elite, the king's officials

---

40 *Babad Tanah Djawi*, p. 252. This was said of Raden Sukra, although the son of the highest official, the grand vizier, in contradiction to the crown prince, who is "son of a king." In another place (p. 251) Raden Sukra is called a "wong tjilik," a commoner.

41 J. F. C. Gericke, *Javaansch-Nederduitsch Woordenboek*, Amsterdam, 1847.

42 Paku Buwana IX, *op. cit.*, p. 173, in the part "Wulang Punggawa."

43 *Ibid.*

44 Paku Buwana IV, *op. cit.*, p. 16.

45 Mangkunagara IV, *op. cit.*, p. 49.

traditionally were recruited mainly from the *prijaji* class, the social group which essentially consisted of the king's *punggawa* (officials) but gradually came to include their families and their descendants. Yet, the essential criterion for membership remained being in the king's service; consequently, if a person were not a *punggawa* his inclusion in the *prijaji* class depended on a close blood-relationship to a royal functionary. The higher the position of a functionary, the longer the line of his descendants included in, or, better, perceived by the community as belonging to this social group. But even the number of royal descendants included in the privilege group was limited. The titles of the *putra* (the king's immediate offspring) and of the *sentana* (the king's extended family) change according to the distance of the relationship; the immediate offspring of the monarch are titled *gusti* and the furthest removed descendants are called *raden*.[46]

Before he could acquire a position in the bureaucratic hierarchy, a young man usually had to go through two phases of instruction, the first of which was the *njuwita* (to serve) and the next, the *magang*-ship (apprenticeship). As a boy of twelve to fifteen years he had to *njuwita*, to serve with a family, usually of a higher standing than his own. He might do ordinary servant's work like sweeping the floor or carrying water but the essence of *njuwita* was always to learn by experience the humility and hardships of a low position in the first place, and to learn by observation the intricacies of higher milieu etiquette in the second place. He was also expected to acquire professional skills (like writing, reading, horse-riding, the use of weapons) and artistic skills (primarily in literature, dance and music).[47]

This procedure of acquiring knowledge and so opening the opportunity to enter officialdom has been a regular practice for all strata of the Javanese society. Ki Padmasusastra (1840-1926), well known because of his knowledge and documentation of Javanese customs and tradition, described in his *Tatatjara* (Traditional Customs) life in a typical Javanese family of his time, from birth to death, not even

---

46 See also: Winter, *Javaansche Zamenspraken*, p. 12.

47 The *Nagarakrtagama* already mentioned that the king himself demonstrated a dance and the princes sang and recited poetry, a reason to conclude that music, dance and literature must be part of the education of a gentleman.

forgetting a favorite pastime, the raising of fighting cocks.[48] In this book the knowledge required of a *prijaji* is of professional skills, the arts and religion; however the art of war is not mentioned at all. Formerly the art of fighting was demonstrated in the colorful contests of skill and courage, the *senenan* (or *seton*, named after the day: Monday and Saturday on which these events were held). The *senenan* was a mock fight with the blunted lance on horseback in the great square before the *kraton* (palace). Ki Padmasusastra's exclusion of the ability to use arms is undoubtedly due to the conditions of his time, when, because of the reduction of the powers of Javanese kings in the nineteenth century, there was no longer the opportunity to display military skill. It is therefore not surprising that Mangkunegara IV, who was allowed by the Netherland-Indies government to have a small but effective contingent of troops, tried to revive the spirit of *ksatria*-ship (knighthood) by stressing in his writings the virtue of *kawirjan* (courageous attitude). For this purpose he empha-sized in his very popular poem *Tripama* (the three examples) the three *ksatrias* of the *wajiang*, Suwanda, Kumbakarna and Surjaputra (Karna) ; each died the death of a true ksatria in a hopeless battle honoring his pledge to fight for his lord even, in the case of the last two heroes, for a morally unjustifiable cause.[49] Prince Mangkunegara IV went so far in his praise that he declared:

> the profession of warrior, that is the highest one ...superseding ascetic practice of a yogi, because the offering of the prayers must be done on top of the iron mountain.[50]

Religious knowledge, of which the ability to recite the complete Kor'an formed an essential part, was considered a further asset in the education of a son of the *prijaji* class. In Ki Padmasusastra's time religious education entailed a rather long stay (three years) at the famed *pesantrens* (or *pondok*: religious school) of Panaraga.[51] The man of religion as the general educator was an ancient institution. The *Serat Rama* mentioned

---

48 Padmasusastra, *Serat Tatatjara*, Semarang, 1911, p. 225.
49 Mangkunegara IV, *op. cit.*, the parts "Pariwijata" and "Tripama."
50 *Ibid.*, p. 50.
51 Padmasusastra, *op. cit.*, p. 173.

the necessity to protect the *panditas* and *resis* (men of religion who lived in contemplative seclusion) with whom the king had to leave his young men to be educated.

You must let them teach what is good in the service of the state.[52]

The phrasing of this statement by Rama to his brother Barata might justify the conclusion that the sages, beside the rules of morality, taught also the techniques of statesmanship contained in the whole body of traditional literature.

After the young man had been educated, his — or his family's — concern would then be to get him as a wife a daughter of a ranking official or better still, of a nobleman, for this to a certain extent would also pave his way to officialdom. Then he must seek admittance to the administration by way of the second apprenticeship or *magang* to a high dignitary, without any pay and for an indefinite time, depending on his capacities and, of course, also on the contacts his family had in the higher echelons of the king's service. From then on, until he reached the highest rank possible, it was required that he consistently show his *kamantepan* or *katemenan* (earnest perseverance, devotion) to the king and to his task, which implied an unquestioning execution of any task which the king commanded him to do. The story of *Dewarutji* was usually used to illustrate such an attitude. Bima, the forceful second Pandawa, unquestion-ingly carried out the orders of his *guru* (teacher) Durna, even when Durna tried to dispose of him (and the threat he would present in the coming Baratajuda war) by sending him to exceedingly dangerous places ostensibly to seek for the truth of life. Bima emerged victoriously, because the gods, struck by his unrelenting perseverance, allowed him to find the truth of life in the middle of the ocean in the form of Dewarutji.[53]

In connection with the devotion required of the *prijaji* by his monarch, it is no more than natural that *seba*, being present on the traditional days of audience, Monday and Thursday (*Senen* and *Kemis*), was thought of as being the servant's most important duty. *Seba* signified the official's

---

52 Jasadipura I, *op. cit.*, p. 41.
53 Prijohoetomo, *op. cit.*, p. 177.

readiness to serve anytime the monarch or his superior demanded it. But the political meaning of the *seba* is even more important, for it was a public show of submission to the authority and rule of a superior. *Seba* was of such essential importance in the formal relationship between superior and subordinate that it was repeatedly mentioned in the *piwulangs* as being of most praiseworthy merit. The *Wulangreh* makes it a duty of all officials, of all ranks.[54] The *Margowirjo* of Djajadiningrat I of Surakarta mentions that the traditional figure of the Prince of Karanggajam in Padjang's times (second half of the sixteenth century) wrote a *kakawin surti*, a kind of didactic poem, which gave advice to those officials who could not afford to live a life of seclusion. The Prince wrote that the place for doing *tapa* (ascetic practice) "within the state" was the *paseban*,[55] the open hall where the king's officials came to *seba*, sitting on their mats, awaiting possible orders from the king. On that very spot officials were expected to do continuous *semedi* (concentration). When one has seen court officials sitting for hours on end in the sand-strewn courtyard of the inner palace compounds in the shadow of the many trees one cannot help but be impressed by their correct, absolute immobility and yet undiminishing alertness; this posture and state of mind was most favorable to the constant spiritual awareness of the *semedi*. The custom of doing pasa *Senen-Kemis*, fasting on the audience days, must also nave a connec-tion with the idea of *semedi* on the *paseban*.

If an official wished to express a grudge, resentment or antipathy against his superior or the king, he would deliberately avoid coming to the *pasowanans* (appearing before the king). For example, when Panembahan Senapati, first ruler of Mataram, decided to stand as an independent ruler, he showed his intention by not coming to his suzerain's audience days.[56] However, if a king granted an official the right, for a defined length of time, to be absent from the audiences, this was deemed a great favor. The regional chie of Priangan (the Sunda highlands of West Java), in his charte of installation from Sultan Agung of Mataram, was allowed "to stay away" from Mataram for "pitung padjenengan" (seven reigns, perhaps meant here as seven years) because of his help in subduing the rebellion of the

---

54 Paku Buwana IV, *op. cit.*, p. 16.

55 R. M. H. Djajadiningrat I, *Margowirjo*, Surakarta, 1908, p. 30.

56 *Babad Tanah Djawi*, pp. 70-72.

adipati of Ukur in 1630.[57] Panembahan Senapati,after his installation as successor to his father as Padjang's vassal, was allowed to be absent from court for one year.[58] One's guess is that this privilege also entailed dispensation from the yearly tributes for the same length of time.

The *pasowanans* had a special function, namely to enhance the glory of the king. On special occasions, like the *Garebeg*, literally all of the king's officials from every part of the country were required to come. The glitter and pomp displayed on these occasions and, certainly not in the least, the great number of persons attending were *perceptible* evidence of the king's greatness and authority. But from the point of view of the officials, to be included in such events was a great honor, particularly as the strict hierarchical arrangement of seating, the distinctive color and pattern of apparel and paraphernalia,and the number of persons in their entourages clearly displayed their exact place in the bureaucratic hierarchy.

The necessity for such perceptible marks of distinction in terms of status, prestige and authority made detailed and precisely defined etiquette an essential part of *prijaji* life. Burger mentions an over-emphasis on refinement at the courts of Javanese kings in the last centuries,[59] but such emphasis was perhaps the result of the fact that ability as the basis of authority could not find its expression in the *political sphere*, at least not in accord with the traditional standards of victorious campaigns and sumptuous gifts.

It was apparent that, in his service to the king, it was expected that the *prijaji* would never be led by personal motives or pecuniary needs.[60] For him, being in the king's service must be a great honor and he should always be ready to sacrifice his possessions or even his life should the welfare of the state or the wish of the king demand it. He must be brave without boasting, alert, earnest and grave,[61] in short a *ksatria* (knight), able to bridle his passions. These are the qualities which differentiated the *ksatria* from the *buta* (ogre) with his unrestrained lusts and greeds.[62] The

57 J. Brandes, "Nog iets over een reeds vroeger gepubliceerde Piagem van Sultan Ageng," *Tijdschrift*, 32, 1889, p. 363

58 *Babad Tanah Djawi*, p. 70.

59 Burger, *op. cit.*, p. 13.

60 *Serat Rama*, p. 37.

61 Paku Buwana IV, *op. cit.*, p. 25.

62 Wedyodipuro, "Het Wajangspel," in *Congres voor Javaansche Cultuur Ontwikkeling*,

prijaji is true to his work, brave beyond doubt, free of selfish motives in his service to the king (*sepi ing pamrih, rame ing gawe*). In his outlook towards life, in his ambitions and ideals, he of course followed closely those of the king, which is natural since, as we have seen, the different levels of the king's administration, although certainly there were gradations of power, in essence followed the same pattern of authority and prestige.[63]

Javanese tradition divides the life of the *prijaji* into three distinctly different phases. The first phase of development (youth) is marked by trial and error, and *lara-lapa* (pain and hunger, suffering). These are the years of *njuwita*, *magang*-ship, and the long stay at the *pesantren* (religious school) under very simple conditions and harsh discipline; it is a period of learning in anticipation of a task in the king's ranks. But there was also the idea that this phase of life should be a life of abandon, tasting all the sweetness of life, an idea which might have been inspired by the examples of Sunan Kalidjaga[64] and Ken Angrok who were notorious highwaymen in their younger years, as was also the robber Djakawana. These three became men of outstanding qualities later, the first becoming a *wali*, the second a king and the third a noted commander of troops. These stories were in turn based on the belief that the *awatāra* (Skrt.: divine incarnation) of god Wisnu, King Krsna, in his youth also led a life of lust and abandon. These stories all describe an abrupt change from bad to good when the hero suddenly becomes aware of his vocation, and consequently is cured of vices (*tobat*). The tales seem to have the same meaning as the initiation rites which in primitive societies mark the change between stages of life.

The second phase of life was characterized by responsibility and the dutiful execution of tasks and also by the achievement of standing and greatness in the material world. Then came the third phase when, after retirement, the *prijaji* took up the contemplation of life's purpose and devoted him-self to the study of the *ngelmu* (mystical knowledge), in general transferring his interest from the material to the spiritual world. He embarked upon this course, not only to prepare himself for the hereafter, but also to enhance the welfare of the world by generating the power of spiritual concentration; moreover, he sought God's consent for

---

Surakarta, 1918.

63 See p . 77 .

64 *Babad Mataram*, Vol. I, p. 19.

his descendants' continuance of his state of *prijaji*-ship. Dr. de Casparis in his inaugural lecture as a professor at Air-langga University in Malang mentions these phases of life in connection with the monarch who had to go through three *asramas* (Old-Jav.: phase of life). In the first *asrama*, the king studied books on religion, law and the life. In the second, he reigned and in the third, he retired and devoted himself to the well-being of the world through the force of contemplation.[65] This is what a king must do if he wants to live according to his *svadharma*, his own destiny. This concept is of Hindu origin.

The Technical Organization of the Administration

The Lord-Vassal Relationship

It is rather difficult to find in Later Mataram literature clear indications of the existence of a formal distinction between the king's nomarchs[66] in the outer regions and the ranking administrators at the capital. As far as rank, title or honors are concerned, there were no differences. Yet the very distinction between core regions and outer territories was and must be based on a real difference between the political status of the two groups of functionaries. A distinction was drawn between the *nagaragung* (the great lands) as the core regions, and the *mantjanegara*[67] (the surrounding or neighboring regions) and the *pasisir* (the coastal provinces) as the outer territories. Such a distinction was made not only in the Later Mataram kingdoms but also in the time of Madjapahit rule when the core regions were divided into vice-royalties under the personal administration of the king's close relatives,[68] his father, mother, cousins, nephews and nieces. The tributaries, all outside Java, were denoted in the Nagarakrtagama as:

> the other islands, all ring-kingdoms, looking for support, numerous...[69]

---

65 De Casparis, *op. cit.*
66 It seems better, instead of using the word vassal, to borrow the more neutral term "nomarch" defined by Rushton Coulborn as "chief officer of local government" (Coulborn, *op. cit.*, p. 5) in order not to get a prejudiced and predetermined view of this institution.
67 Veth, *op. cit.*, p. 575; *Babad Tanah Djawi*, pp. 81, 87.
68 Pigeaud, *Java in the 14th Century*, Vol. IV, p. 10.
69 *Ibid.*, Vol. III, p. 15.

The reference to the "ring-kingdoms," as Pigeaud translates *mandalita rastra*,[70] is rather interesting as that term might be interpreted as having exactly the same connotation as the word *mantjanegara* and might be similarly related to the analogous *mantjapat* and *mantjalima* village alliances we have mentioned before.[71]

When and how the distinction between core and outer regions became established in the Later Mataram period is not known. The region of Mataram proper had been granted by Sultan Adiwidjaja of Padjang (1568-1586) to Kyageng Pemanahan, founder of the House of Mataram, as an unexploited area which "is still forest"[72] which means that it was still sparsely populated, while Pati, given to Ki Pandjawi by the Sultan, was already a "negari," a populated town. This does indicate that, at that time, there were still territories available, exploited or unexploited, which could be distributed as territorial grants to the followers of the king over which they obtained full rights of disposal and administration and where they would actually reside. Although Mataram is only fifty miles away from the capital of Padjang it apparently was not considered part of the core region, the region which in later times would include all appanages of royal dignitaries residing in the capital just as it did in the Madja-pahit times. Living in the capital would, to a certain extent, hamper the officials in the exercise of their full autonomous rights. Perhaps Mataram was in a fully autonomous position during Padjang times because the king did not strictly follow the policy of keeping his officials close to himself by providing them with appanages within the core region.[73] Only the later kings of Mataram strictly adhered to such a policy and it forced them to enlarge the core region until, towards the end of the eighteenth century, it included the Bagelen-Kedu area and the Jogjakarta-Surakarta area.[74] Another explanation of the growth of the core region might be that as a result of greater elaboration in court life a greater number of officials was required and with the appanage system of salaries the area of available land simply had to be expanded.

---

70 *Ibid.*, Vol. I, p. 10, Canto 12.6.4.

71 See p. 27.

72 *Babad Tanah Djawi*, p. 59.

73 Some appanages of court dignitaries, as an exception, were outside the core region, for instance in Patjitan and Blitar.

74 Rouffaer, *op. cit.*, p. 4.

Although an official resided in the capital, his duties were not necessarily limited to the court or the inner regions. Many had jurisdiction over territories or affairs outside the core regions, as commander of troops, as controllers of revenue in the coastal provinces or in the maintenance of relations with the outside world. However, not very much is known about the jurisdictions of the central functionaries. For instance, it is not known how far the authority of the grand vizier extended relative to the inner and to the outer regions.

Nomarchs residing in the outer regions, and so outside the Nagaragung, undoubtedly had more freedom of movement; they were under less control simply because of the distance from court. Most of these outer regions were under the administration of the local nobility; these included territories which had been formerly more or less independent from Mataram, like Surabaja, Tuban, Kediri, and Ukur in West Java, and territories which formerly had been administered locally by dignitaries appointed by the court, like Banjumas (Pasir) and also Mataram itself during the reign of the kings of Demak and Padjang in the fifteenth and sixteenth centuries.[75] It was also the case with Madiun and Pati.[76] The main duties of the regional officers were collecting the yearly payment of revenue for the king's treasury and supplying manpower for war or for building public utilities like roads and canals.

In terms of authority and power of the king's nomarchs, for the regions more or less directly to the north of Mataram proper, another policy was followed. There was considerable involvement of the court in the administration of these *"pasisir"* territories, probably because they were located on the road to the north coast of Java, the gateway to foreign political and economic relations. At one time Pekalongan (1623), Djepara (1733 and 1737), and Banjumas (1737), the last to the west of Mataram, were governed — via a local representative — by a court dignitary at the capital.[77] Schrieke called Pekalongan an appanage of a court dignitary. Furthermore, the importance of the harbors of Djepara, Lasem, Djuana

75 Pigeaud, *Java in the 14th Century*, Vol. IV, p. 375. For the later period see *Babad Tanah Djawi*, p. 158.

76 The great rebellion of *adipati* Pragola against Sultan Agung attested to the independent position of this local power-holder. (De Graaf, *Geschiedenis*, p. 110; *Babad Tanah Djawi*, pp. 110-111.)

77 Schrieke, *op. cit.*, Vol. II, pp. 192, 169.

and later, Semarang, to foreign trade and relations demanded a rather different administration. Here the *sahbandars* or harbor-masters formed a new element in state adminis-tration. The *Babad Tanah Djawi* mentions the *adipati* Sura Adimenggala, who was made the administrator of

> the village-lands along the main highway, going from Semarang to Kartasura.[78]

This was in 1703 and the creation of this function undoubtedly was meant to meet the needs of the time.

With all these examples of the realities of administration in mind, hard and fast rules cannot be drawn about the competencies and powers of the dignitaries administering the two main parts of the realm, for there was always a fluidity of situation and an ever-changing balance of power. Kingship in Java was characterized by the all-importance of personal relationships and thus the balance of power was entirely dependent on the personalities of and relations between the holders of power at the capital and in the regions or between the regional nomarchs themselves.[79]

So during the Later Mataram period the king's administration was essentially an hierarchical line of separate, self-sufficient and highly autonomous units of power, vertically linked by the direct and personal ties between the several power-holder/administrators. Apart from the binding ties of a common servitude and loyalty, there did not seem to be any horizontal administrative relationship which could limit the monarchs' independence from each other. In fact, high-handed acts of violence towards fellow nomarchs were apt to occur when the controlling power of the central authority was lacking. This was made all the more tempting because the nomarchs' autonomy entailed the right to have their own armed forces.[80] It was therefore very usual that when an official would go into rebellion, he would first attack the neighboring region.[81] Raden Rangga Prawiradirdja III, Jogjakarta's *bupati* (regional head) of the Madiun region at about the beginning of the nineteenth century, on his own

---

78 *Babad Tanah Djawi*, p. 278.
79 See also Schrieke, *op. cit.*, Vol. II, p. 207.
80 *Babad Tanah Djawi*, pp. 136, 324.
81 *Ibid.*, pp. 110, 114, 308.

initiative plundered some villages in the Surakarta region of Panaraga.[82] The Chief-regent of Madiun reported an attack on his residency by the regent of Muneng and his son.[83] The nomarchs' independence can also be seen from the alliances of regional officials to rise against their king, notably that of the regional chief of Madura, Pangeran Tjakraningrat, and of Surabaja, *tumenggung* Djajengrana of Surabaja, during the reign of AmangKurat III (1703-1708),[84] in support of Pangeran Puger, later Paku Buwana I.

The self-sufficiency of function and the preponderant position of chiefs on all levels of the administration contributed to the repetitive character of the administration's organizational set-up.[85] The *patih* (vizier) was the head of the executive, overseer and coordinator of the administrative departments' fulfillment of his master's orders. Important functionaries at court and regional administrators alike had their own *patih*, sometimes two, a *patih ndjero* and a *patih ndjaba* (inner and outer *patih*) in imitation of the King's court where one *patih* was responsible for court affairs and one for the administration of the realm. The two prominent governors of Surabaja had two *patihs* each.[86] The *Babad Tanah Djawi* mentions the *patih* of Pangeran Puger, who later became grand vizier of Mataram when his master ascended the throne as Paku Buwana I (1703-1719).

Ki Setradjaja, *patih* of the Kapugeran principality, was made grand vizier, governing the people of entire Java, and he was granted [by the king] the name adipati Tjakradjaja. Ki Banjak Patra was made inner-*patih*, and granted the name tumenggung Kartanegara.[87]

---

82 L. Adam, "Geschiedkundige aanteekeningen omtrent de residentie Madioen," *Djawa*, Vol. 20 (1940), nos. 4-5, p. 334. See also Schrieke, *op. cit.*, Vol. II, p. 219, citing a report of Governor General J. P. Coen (1619-1623 and 1627-1628).

83 T. Roorda, *Javaansch Brievenboek*, Leiden, 1904 p. 132.

84 *Babad Tanah Djawi*, p. 266.

85 The term "repetitive" is preferable to "imitative" because in the idea of the macro/micro-cosmic relationship it indicates more a conveyance, magic transfer of essence- -and thus also of form — which made it essential that the receiving substance be of equal capacity, and so, of equal structure. The word *anggaduh*, with its ordinary meaning of "receiving in land-lease," used in connection with power and authority had the connotation indicated above. An example is in the law "Angger Pradata Akir" in which the monarch transferred (*nggaduhake*) for the time being, to do justice to a special dignitary, (Oudemans, *op. cit.*, p. 22.) Similarity in structure of administration is thus more than mere imitation. See also p. 77.

86 Rothenbuhler, *op. cit.*, p. 14.

87 *Babad Tanah Djawi*, p. 279.

A *patih* of a *bupati* at court, Tumenggung Wiraguna, is mentioned in the *Pranatjitra*.[88] Veth confirmed that the *tumeng-gungs* at the end of the nineteenth century also had *patihs*. The Grand Vizier himself seemed to have a *patih* of his own.[89] According to Veth these *patihs* of officials were not considered formally to be officers of the king, which in a sense again reflects the autonomous character of administrative units.

Another similarity between the court administration and those of the nomarchs was in the number of functionaries. The *Pranatjitra* tells that Tumenggung Wiraguna, one of the heroes in the suppression of the revolt of Adipati Pragola of Pati in 1627, had 12 *mantris* (lower officials) under his *patih*. Rouffaer claims that in 1733 there were at court 12 *wedana* (officials of high rank) under the Grand Vizier. Whether the total number of 12 district heads (called *wedana* too) under the two Bupatis of Surabaja (each had six) around 1800[90] imitated the 12 *wedanas* at court in the eighteenth century, is open to conjecture, because at the beginning of the nineteenth century the number of *wedanas* at court had been reduced to eight.

The regional administrations imitated the court in employing public prosecutors. At the end of the nineteenth century, the Grand Vizier employed a *djeksa nagara* (public prosecutor) as did all the eight *wedanas*. The *djeksas* of the *wedanas* and those of dignitaries heading special departments of administration formed the Pradata court[91] which was presided over by the *djeksa nagara*. Moreover, just as at the capital, regional *bupatis* had their own *pengulu* (head of the clergy).

Officials seem to have had full autonomy in the appointment of subordinates and apparently also in the apportionment of territories of jurisdiction to them. The *demangs* (chiefs over some villages), for instance, were appointed by that official whose appanage included the area of the *demang*.[92] And the Chief-regent of Madiun, Kandjeng Pangeran Rangga Harja Prawiradiningrat, proposed at one time that the Dutch Resident of Surakarta appoint his candidate to the post of *bupati* of Gorang-gareng, and also confirm his intention of joining the regency of Muneng with

88 *Pranatjitra*, Batavia, 1932, p. 9.0
89 Veth, *op. cit.*, p. 589.
90 Rothenbuhler, *op. cit.*, p. 15.
91 Winter, "Regtspleging," p. 103.
92 Roorda, *op. cit.*, p. 38.

another district.[93] Although apparently the consent of the Dutch Resident was necessary — this was in 1813 — this example gives us some idea of the extent of the authority of the king's officials for their respective regions. Given the repetitive character of administration, this might also have been true of lower officials in their own territorial or personal jurisdictions.

One can understand that these units of administration posed a potential danger to the unity of the state, for each of them was a complete and similarly organized entity. A favorable change in the power relationships or an ambitious and bold leader could propel it into an independent position or attempt to seize the superior position. Paku Buwana IX's warnings to his kinsmen are telling.

> Please, my descendants, do not try and reach for the crown ... because if you intend to become a king, your wish will not find its mark.

He then suggested a rather inadequate substitute.

> On the other hand, place yourself under the favor of the one who is chosen crown prince, and if you have a child, of beautiful countenance, pray that she will be his spouse...[94]

It was therefore essential for the king to keep a close and unrelenting watch over his *prijajis*, whether they were persons of his own blood or the landed nobility of the outer regions incorporated into his realm, or commoners who had risen into the *prijaji* class. In the eight ideal characteristics of the king, the ability to "see the movement of body and soul of his officials" (*mawas obah osiking bala*) was ascribed to the god Baju.[95] Such an attitude did not contradict the requirement that the king should fully trust his officials, because such vigilance was primarily meant to detect any slight intention of standing up against his author ity and was not intended to curb the official's authority in his own field. Naturally such

---

93 *Ibid.*, p. 174.
94 Paku Buwana IX, *op. cit.*, p. 85.
95 Jasadipura I, *op. cit.*, pp. 434, 436.

control had to be exercised secretly. The word *mata-pitaja* (lit. "trusted-eye") for the secret investigator and *lampah sandi* for "doing in secret" attested to this widely used practice. Javanese tradition demanded from a responsible official that he know everything happening in his territory, and it was usual that at certain times he made rounds during the night with an armed escort (*nganglang*) to investigate the state of security and contentment in his district. If the situation demanded he would also mingle among the people incognito (*njamur kawula*) to inform himself of public opinion.

In order to maintain control over his subordinates, the king resorted to three methods.[96] The first was the use of harsh force, even to the extent of executing possible contenders and their family, a method which was by no means rarely applied. Schrieke mentions that probably Panembahan Senapati had to eliminate the local ruling family before he could sit securely on the Mataram throne.[97] The House of Pati and that of Adipati Ukur of West Java were destroyed after their revolt. Sultan Agung also eliminated the local nobility of Madura except that of Sampang,[98] and the family of the ecclesiastical lord of Giri was reduced to virtual extinction in 1680 by Mataram's forceful methods.[99]

A second method of central control was the practice of keeping influential regional dignitaries at court for long periods of time while their provinces were left to the care of their representatives. Pangeran Tjakraningrat of Madura and Adipati Djajengrana of Surabaja were so powerful that Amangkurat II called them "the bulwark of the kingdom of Mataram,"[100] and they virtually lived in Mataram. Before them the Senapati of Kediri and later Pangeran Pekik of Sura-baja stayed in Mataram too,[101] presumably to ensure the loyalty of their people to Mataram's ruler. But one event showed that such a policy might also be fatal. Raden Truna-djaja, on the instigation of the Crown Prince himself, stood up against Mataram and managed without difficulty to subjugate the Madura region,

---

96 See Schrieke, *op. cit.*, Vol. II, Book II, Sec. IV.

97 One will remember in Burmese history the almost traditional bloodbaths to eliminate all possible competitors when a ruler came to the throne.

98 Schrieke, *op. cit.*, Vol. II, p. 218.

99 De Graaf, *Geschiedenis*, p. 224.

100 *Babad Tanah Djawi*, p. 242.

101 *Ibid.*, p. 108, 134.

while the regional head was staying at court.[102]

The third method was alignment through marriage. The marriage of Panembahan Senapati to princess Djuminah of Madiun, a descendant of the kings of Demak, Sultan Agung's marriage to the daughter of Tjirebon's Panembahan Ratu, and the marriage of the Sultan's sister, Ratu Pandansari, to the prince of Surabaja, Pangeran Pekik, are well-known examples of such a policy. Also, the custom of *triman* (lit.: what was received), the king giving a princess in marriage to his officials of rank, served the same purpose. Some writers see the *prijaji* practice of taking concubines from among the commoners as an attempt to strengthen the bonds between princely nobility and the people.[103] But the practice owed more, presumably, to the king's prerogative to choose his mate at will than to the serious intention of establishing ties of kinship between high and low.

The possibility that commoners might rise to high officialdom also served to reduce the dangers of an established aristocracy; the new elite, grateful for their newly acquired status and thus more trustworthy, counterbalanced the blood aristocracy. Perhaps the followers' simultaneous rise in rank when the master obtained a position of importance, of which instances are easily found in the *Babad Tanah Djawi*, was also rooted in the master's quest for security by encircling himself with a group of trusted followers.[104] And we know that instant reward for demonstrated merit was considered a good royal policy.[105] It was inevitable that the state administration be primitively organized, permitting the existence of almost independent regional units tied only by personal attachments and loyalties, because the regions were far-flung and communications poor.[106] However, the danger of disintegration was inherent in the system, especially as hereditary succession stimulated the establishment of new gentry families.

The right to inherit one's father's position was well known and became established as a custom in the last centuries of Later Mataram, although

---

102 *Ibid.*, p. 157.
103 B. ter Haar, *Adat Law in Indonesia*, New York, 1948, p. 76.
104 *Babad Tanah Djawi*, pp. 261, 279.
105 See p. 69.
106 Schrieke, *op. cit.*, Vol. II, Book II, One, 3 and 4.

presumably neither the extent of territorial jurisdiction nor the extent of appanages received as remuneration for his services to the king was assured. These remained the prerogative of the king or the regional chief. The Madiun regency seemed especially subject to frequent reparceling, and even at one time (1755) the small Madiun district of Gorang-gareng was a regency.[107] Tjaruban and Djagaraga were also small regencies. The Pangeran of Lamongan, after the revolt of Trunadjaja (1677-1680), was given a *lungguh* (appanage) which the king had taken from (*kagempalaken*: broken off) the territory of Surabaja.[108] Even a prince could not be assured an appanage. Amangkurat IV (1719-1727) deprived Pangeran Blitar of his appanage, the region of Blora.[109] The whimsicality of the king in handing out even the highest positions is evident in the *Babad Tanah Djawi* story of Amangkurat I's raising a son of *ki bujut* (alderman) Kalawejan, (the title is of a low, relatively unimportant rank) to the rank of *bupati* of Semarang, only because on a sea voyage, when the king felt thirsty, the *ki bujut* happened to be able to serve him refreshing fruits.[110]

According to an account of conditions in Surakarta in the mid-1880's inheritance of a "*kalungguhan*" (function, from *lungguh*: appanage) came, in order of precedence, to the:

1. eldest son, although precedence was given to a son of the main-wife; and then to the other sons;
2. eldest daughter, who would be represented by her husband, for the benefit of her eldest son (whether the other daughters had preference above the next group is not certain);
3. brothers, father's brothers, nephews along the patrilineal line, cousins along the patrilineal line;

or "that which was preferred by the government"[111] which means that royal caprice had the ultimate say. This might mean that, in principle,

---

107 Roorda, *op. cit.*, p. 171.
108 *Babad Tanah Djawi*, p. 197.
109 *Ibid.*, p. 334.
110 *Ibid.*, p. 198.
111 Winter, *Javaansche Zamenspraken*, p. 13.

functions were not hereditary and, since the aristocracy mainly was identified with function in the king's administration, aristocracy was in principle not hereditary either.

The account also mentions non-hereditary functions, namely that of the *raden adipati* (the title of the grand vizier), the *pengulu* (head of the clergy) and the *djeksa* (public prosecutor). Reasons for these exceptions are not given. The positions of Grand Vizier and *patih* were held by the master's most trusted follower or right-hand man; their selection very much depended on personal considerations. Nevertheless, hereditary tendencies can be detected even for these positions.[112]

Territorial Division of the Realm

It is interesting to note that the Javanese, apparently from olden times on, had almost always identified the state with the king's residence. One can hardly find any example in which the name of the state was not that of the capital. Kadiri, Singhasari, Madjapahit, Padjang, Demak, Surakarta, Jogjakarta all derived their names from their respective capitals. Some, like Mataram and Bintara, were named after the regions where the kingdoms were originally established. Cosmologically, the capital as residence of the king formed the magical center of the realm[113] but also, from the viewpoint of state politics, the central region was preponderantly important. We have already seen evidence of a center-oriented outlook in administrative organization; the core region was relatively closely knit through the use of a remuneration system of appanages, while the outer regions were more loosely administered.

The physical powers of the state, notably the core regiments of the armed forces, were concentrated in the capital; the army went out to the regions to demonstrate the king's ability to subjugate or quell revolts, but always returned to the capital. This fact indicates a center-oriented view. Armed forces were never occupational, but always expedi-tional.[114]

---

112 See also Th. Pigeaud, "K. P. Arja Adipati Danoeredja VII," *Djawa*, Vol. 11 (1931), no. 4, p. 128ff.

113 Heine-Geldern, *op. cit.*, p. 3.

114 *Babad Tanah Djawi*, pp. 107, 109.

The contradistinction of the three kinds of regions seen from the position of the center attests also to this view. In the *Nagarakrtagama* we find three territorial provinces: Java, the regions and islands outside Java including the southern part of the Malay peninsula, and the countries beyond, like Champa and Cambodia.[115] In the Later Mataram period there were also three categories, *nagaragung* (the core region), *mantjanegara* and the *pasisir* (the outlying provinces), and the *tanah sabrang* (the lands across the sea). This territorial concept is in accord with Professor Veth's and Dr. Selosoemardjan's observations that the Javanese states were laid out in concentric circles,[116] beginning with the innermost circle of the palace and ending with the outermost territories. What we have observed about the relative position of officials in the *nagaragung* and in the *mantjanegara*[117] leads us to conclude that a territory was allocated to one of the three categories on the basis of the degree of influence that the center, that is, the king, exercised there. Consequently, territorial jurisdiction could not be strictly defined by permanent boundaries, but was characterized by a fluidity or flexibility of boundary dependent on the diminishing or increasing power of the center. This was evident in the words of the *dalang* cited elsewhere; the state "is far-reaching in its fame,"[118] and was a "bright world." The state is thus likened to a torch so bright that it spreads its light far afield. It is rather difficult to find a clear indication of how this concept of territory as spheres of influence affected state policy. However, evidence of the concept might be seen in the circular expansion of the original region of Mataram (the districts "Mataram" and perhaps also "Gading Mataram"[119]) into the core region, the "Nagara-gung," of later days, and further in the existence of appanages outside the *nagaragung* which were called the appanages of the *djabarangkah*[120] (outside the boundaries). The gradual shrinkage of the Mataram regions because of loss to the Dutch characteristically also followed this pattern of concentric circles, in the sense that it diminished from the outermost

---

115 Pigeaud, *Java in the 14th Century*, Vol. IV, p. 35.
116 Veth, *op. cit.*, Vol. II, p. 575; Selosoemardjan, *op. cit.*, p. 24.
117 See p. 86.
118 See p. 61.
119 Rouffaer, *op. cit.*, pp. 4, 53.
120 *Ibid.*, p. 7.

to the more inner circles of state territory.[121]

To assume, however, that territorial claim was not important is wrong. The very distinction between *nagaragung* and *mantjanegara* indicates that the king had a stronger ter-ritorial claim in the former than in the latter part of the realm. The apportioning of appanages outside the core region, and also the establishment of colonies by Sultan Agung mentioned in de Haan's well-known work on the Priangan region, namely, among others, that of 2000 men under Kyai Singapra-bangsa along the Tjimanuk river in 1653, are examples of territory claimed by dint of settlement by royal subjects, thus through personal jurisdiction. De Haan based his view of the importance of personal jurisdiction on the fact that untilled soil had no value at all in an agrarian society.[122] However, a passage in the *Babad Tanah Djawi* does not seem to confirm the idea of territorial claim through one's subjects. When Panembahan Senapati (1575-1601) planned to attack the *bang wetan* (the eastern parts of Java as distinct from the *bang kulon*, the western part of Java seen from Mataram), the regional chiefs of Tuban, Sedaju, Lamongan, Gresik, Lumadjang, Kertasana, Malang, Pasuruhan, Kediri, Wirasaba, Blitar, Pringga-baja, Pragunan, Lasem, Madura, Sumenep and Pakatjangan, under the leadership of Pangeran Surabaja, formed a grand alliance to withstand the attack. The religious leader of Giri tried to persuade the parties to avoid war by having the two opponents, Panembahan Senapati and Pangeran Surabaja, choose via an envoy between "the content and the receptacle" (*isi lan wadah*) in order to determine who would be "high" and who would be "low." Senapati allowed Pangeran Surabaja to choose first and he chose the "content." Upon hearing this, Sunan Giri declared

> Let it be known that it is determined by God's Will that Senapati has rightly reserved the receptacle for himself. The receptacle is the realm, the content, the people. If the people would not obey the one who owns the land, they will be ousted.[123]

Such a statement seems to raise the importance of territory above that of

---

121 See Map I.
122 F. de Haan, *Priangan*, Batavia, 1910, Vol. I, p. 15.
123 *Babad Tanah Djawi*, pp. 99-100.

the people as the king's subjects. However, Sunan Giri's ruling should be seen more in the context of the fluidity of spheres of influence discussed above; jurisdiction, be it personal or territorial, had to be expanded or retracted according to the reality of power distribution between powerholders in the center and the regions as well as between different states.

Boundaries were known. They consisted of waterways, mountains and mountain ranges,[124] natural divisions which were very convenient as border indicators. The intention to mark off territories as permanent political units and thus to ward off jurisdictional disputes was almost unattainable because of the fluidity of power relations. During Airlangga's reign (1019-1049), Mpu Bharada was to create with magic water an "uncrossable" division of Java into two parts, Pandjalu (Kadiri) and Djanggala.[125] Interestingly, Mpu Bharada could not finish his work and so the coming of a dispute was foretold and indeed dispute later arose. So even this tale seems to imply the futility of permanent territorial divisions. Such an intended sanctity of a boundary line perhaps left its traces in the Later Mataram belief that when two opposing armies face each other across a river, the one crossing first will lose the battle.

> It was told of the taboos of the people of old that, when people confront each other in battle, he who crosses the river will certainly lose the battle.[126]

Disobeying this taboo was thought to be the cause of the death of Arja Djipang, pretender to the Demak throne, in about 1570.

The fact that territorial boundaries of the state were fluid did not prevent regions and districts from being well defined geographically if not politically, for recognized natural boundaries were abundant, not the least of which were exceptionally large trees like the *randu alas* (bombax mala-baricum), the wild kapok tree. Natural boundaries are frequently used in the *Babad Tanah Djawi* as landmarks to indicate a region or district: *sawetaning gunung Lawu* (east of the Lawu mountain); *siti dusun*

124 Schrieke, *op. cit.*, Vol. II, p. 104.
125 De Graaf, *Geschiedenis*, p. 51.
126 *Babad Tanah Djawi*, p. 56.

salere redi Kendeng (village lands north of the Kendeng range);[127] also *Padjang kulon Benawi, Sokawati wetan Benawi* (Padjang west of the River, Sokawati east of the River) indicate the location of these areas with respect to the Bengawan Solo. Natural boundaries also played an important part in the Javanese ecological ideal of state territory as it is expressed in the *wajang*.

> *pasir-wukir* ...*pasir* means sea, *wukir*, mountain; because Mandaraka is a kingdom with mountains behind, rice-fields on the left and a great river on the right side, and, in front, it has a large harbor.[128]

Needless to say such an ideal had its political and its economic aspects as well, for sea, river and mountains form natural barriers against invasion, and harbors and ricefields were the basic elements of prosperity.

Before finishing this discussion of the division of the realm we should deal with the territorial importance of the *lungguh* (appanage) in the administration of the state. From our previous discussion and the available literature concerning land rights of the Later Mataram monarchs, we must conclude that the king had two kinds of rights over the land. The first can be called political or public rights for they determine the extent of his territorial jurisdiction. These rights only define the limits or boundaries of the area within which he may administer, that is, in which he may render justice and which he may defend against attack from an enemy.

The second and more direct right of the king vis-a-vis the land is the right to dispose of the *produce* of the soil according to customary law. The basis of the right of disposal seems to be the old village custom (*paron*) of dividing the produce of the soil into half for the tiller of the soil and half for the person who has the right of usufruct, a right which he receives from the *desa* which is the true owner of the land, the *siti dusun* (*desa* land). Although further study is necessary to prove this point, it is not at all improbable that the king's right to the produce of land had developed from this custom. With Professor van Vollenhoven, one can

---

127 *Babad Tanah Djawi*, pp. 257, 110.
128 Tjan Tjoe Siem, *op. cit.*, p. 3.

say that unquestionably the king did not possess the land in the sense of private property; he possessed only the right to a part of the produce of the land which he might farm out to financiers. For however arbitrary the king might have been in the disposal of the right to the produce of the land, the peasant who actually worked the land always received a greater part, originally perhaps 50% of the yield. Rouffaer's suggestion that in the outer regions the king adhered to the old custom of a five-part division of the product of the land in which the people got the largest part, namely two-fifths, or 40%,[129] supports our argument. However, one should not forget that the king, because of his absolute powers, not infrequently violated these traditions, but this does not eliminate the tenability of the principle.

Although the king granted others rights to a portion of the produce of the land, he extracted a certain amount of this portion for his own benefit in the form of a *padjeg* (tax). He thus shared the income of the land with his offi-cers, in the *mantjanegara* with the regional chief (the *Bupati*) and his subordinates (the district heads and the headmen of villages), and in the core region with his appanage-holders and their *bekels* (steward and representative of the appanage-holder in the *desa*).

Two types of landholdings were not liable to the same sort of taxation, namely the *narawita* (crown domains) and the *perdikan* lands, mentioned elsewhere.[130] The crown domains were placed directly under the management of the king through a special official (*wedana midji, midji* denoting a special task or position). These lands were not actually free of tax, but they were reserved entirely for the benefit of the ruler and had to supply commodities like rice,[131] oil, flowers, *suruh* leaves[132] (for betelnut chewing) for the special use of the king's household. Analogously, the regional heads of the outer regions also reserved domains for their own use. For instance, the regents of Surabaja, Rothenbuhler reported, had

---

129 Rouffaer, *op. cit.*, p. 73. The produce of the taxable lands was divided as follows: two-fifths to the tiller; one-fifth to the village chief; and two-fifths to the king, which was divided, one-fifth to his vassal *bupati*, one-fifth to his vassal's officers, and three-fifths to his own treasury (which is 24% of the whole amount). See further Appendix II.

130 See p. 84.

131 Rouffaer, *op. cit.*, p. 51.

132 Roorda, *op. cit.*, p. 28.

their "own lands and villages."[133]

As for land rights given by the king or regional power holders to their officials as a remuneration and also as the means of financing their tasks, we have to distinguish between the *lungguh* (appanage) and the *bengkok* or *tjatu* (salary-fields). Van Vollenhoven defined the appanage as "an assigned region where one has the right to gain from the land and the inhabitants a profit, from which the king can draw (taxes, services, incomes from domains), but which gives no rights on the land itself." A "salary-field" was "a piece of arable land which is part of the lands of the king and assigned to an official, kinsman or a favored person. It is tilled by levy-service to the benefit of the person granted."[134] It is not clear what is meant by the king's lands in the second definition. Formerly, the size of an appanage seemed to be as vast as the territorial jurisdiction the appanage holder was entitled to by dint of his office or rank; later on, however, the appanages became much smaller and more and more they grew to resemble "salary-fields" in size if not in other characteristics, Rouffaer gives examples from 1744 to illustrate the later development.[135]

The appanage system was in effect in the *nagaragung*,for all officials of the court from the highest to the lowest and it existed also for some regional heads in the other provinces. The "salary-field" system was in effect in the *mantjanegara*.[136] An explanation of the difference between the two salary systems — because that was what they essentially were — cannot be easily discovered, nor has it been determined whether the *bengkok* system was applied in all parts of the *mantjanegara* or only in the regions of eastern Java. Besides the appanages and "salary-fields," the king also had his own tax territories, the *siti pamadjegan-dalem*, from which he gathered taxes and labor services for his own benefit.

In the nineteenth century, an official might hold appanages in widely scattered areas. After the 1755 partition, the mixing of appanages caused much incessant bickering between the subjects of Surakarta and

---

133 This kind of special taxation for the use of the court was already old. The *Babad Tjirebon* narrates that, because of the Islamization of Tjirebon, it stopped pay ing tribute of fish paste to Padjadjaran. (*Babad Tjirebon*, p. 15.)

134 Rothenbuhler, *op. cit.*, p. 19.

135 Rouffaer, *op. cit.*, p. 74, see also pp. 76-77.

136 Van Vollenhoven, *op. cit.*, pp. 52, 53.

Jogjakarta, so much so that the situation came to be called the *perang desa* (village wars). It eventually had to be regulated by law.[137]

The shrinkage of the two kingdoms contributed to the fragmentation of landholdings. A district or even a *desa* might be divided into several appanages. At one time it was reported that an average-sized village might be divided into four or six different holdings; larger villages might be divided into ten or more.[138] Landholdings came to be so fragmented that there were many *bekels* (the representatives and tax collectors of the appanage-holder) who did not have a single villager under them and were therefore called *bekel gundul* (bald *bekels*). They were, in fact, their masters'*bekel* and the tillers of the soil. There were many *bekels*, often several in the same village in the core regions of Jogjakarta and Surakarta, who had administrative functions. Thus village heads were seriously challenged in their roles, so much so that in 1896 in Surakarta and sometime later in Jogjakarta their position had to be reinstated.[139]

If we look again at the definition of an appanage it is obvious that it entailed territorial rights, which was also apparent from the right of the appanage-holder to appoint his own *bekel* as his representative and tax collector. The *bekel*, in turn, was given a small appanage by his master. It might be assumed that the appanage system was an older institution than the *bengkok* system; for the latter system had more the character of a simple remuneration for services rendered, while in the appanage there were traces of administrative rights. The system of *lungguh* is thus more in accordance with the repetitive character in the old Javanese state system.

---

137 Law "Angger Gunung," arts. 65, 81, 89, 90. Law "Angger Ageng," art. 22. (Oudemans, *op. cit.*, Vol. II.)
138 Rouffaer, *op. cit.*, p. 85.
139 *Ibid.*, p. 89.

CHAPTER FOUR
CONCLUSION

Before presenting a review of and some conclusions about state and state craft in the Later Mataram period we would like to point again to the main distinction drawn in this study, that between the magico-religious aspect and the technical-economic aspect of kingship.

Belief and religion dominates Javanese society, and kingship in the Later Mataram period drew its strongest support from religious belief. It can even be said that the basis of kingship lay in religion; the authority of the gods justified the authority of the king. The state was seen as an image of, or stronger still, was identified with the divine realm, in its immaterial and in its material aspect. The king, and to a lesser degree his officials as the extension of his power, had to possess might and power commensurate with that of the gods; he had to display the material grandeur and pomp worthy of an image of the gods, and also a lavish beneficence proper to mankind's helper and protector in times of distress. However, to explain the absolute and all-dominating power of the king, we must look to religious conceptions other than the idea that the king's powers must mirror the powers of the deities. For Javanese religion's acceptance of an upper god also served as a means of justifying the king as the absolute and sole power holder in the earthly realm. After the coming of Islam when the god-king identification could no longer be accepted, the absolute powers of the king were made acceptable by making him the only medium between man and God; he became God's spokesman and so his will had God's sanction.

In the magico-religious sphere of kingship the concept of continuity had such great importance that Javanese tradition created two major devices to deal with this problem. A genealogy was created to link preceding dynasties to the present one; deliberate forgery and artificial construction overcame obstacles to the much desired end. Second, the idea was accepted that God's consent in the form of a perceptible token, the *wahju*, was passed from ruler to ruler as the sign of royalty. Similar or identical experiences, as in the well known Ken Angrok-Wisnu identification, also created continuity between rulers. The strong adherence to the principle of continuity was a response to the need to justify new ruling dynasties. The practice of proving continuity might ultimately be rooted in the custom of claiming an inheritance through blood lineage which obviously is the strongest and most ancient way to claim rights, except perhaps for the claim to rights by sheer force.

Strangely enough, claim by force is not unknown in a tradition of such sophistication and refinement as the Javanese. It was expressed in the ceremony of enthronement of a new king, when the king's champions challenged those who would show their opposition to the new monarch's rule.

Such primitiveness as is evident in the idea of kingly authority also appears in the technical and economic implementation of Later Mataram state life. State administration was intrinsically primitive in character. The importance of physical power apparent in the idolization of *ksatria*-ship, the simplicity of administration with its repetitive schema of identical structures, the nondifferentiation of functions in leader positions, the autonomous self-sufficiency of functions, very obvious in its system of finance: all these factors reveal the basic simplicity of concept in the Later Mataram state.[1] Simplicity of structure along with the granting of great personal power and responsibility to each position in the hierarchy might be sufficiently effective as the basic elements of rule in a small territory where central control can be enforced. But in a state of some size, the autonomous position of regional leaders and power holders presented problems; the danger of disintegration was ever present from regional chiefs who felt themselves strong enough to resist the powers of the central authority and to stand on their own, or even worse, to seize the throne for themselves.

Devices to maintain the unity of the state were therefore of overwhelming importance. The outstanding device was the requirement

---

1 See also: Coulborn, *op. cit.*, p. 197.

of schooling in and pursuance of high moral standards as a prerequisite to participation in the king's and — through identification — in God's rule of mankind. The *prijaji*'s belief that his was a highly honorable duty was to a considerable degree responsible for the strong *esprit de corps* among the members of the Javanese ruling elite. Group solidarity was the more enhanced by a second device, intermarriage, which reinforced the strong personal relationships necessary to hold together such an essentially loose organization of the state.

It is evident that in this method of government the personal characteristics of the holders of power at the center as well as in the regions very much determined the stability and efficiency of state life,and the history of the Later Mataram period has shown how disruptive of stability any intrusion could be. The natural balance of power between a strong center and the dependent regional powers was very vulnerable to disturbances,for the regional powers were potentially capable of independence from the center. The effectiveness of such a system of government thus depended on mutual respect and, ultimately, on the persuasiveness of physical force.

BIBLIOGRAPHY

Adam, L. "Geschiedkundige aanteekeningen omtrent de residentie Madioen," *Djawa*, Vol. 20 (1940), nos. 4-5.

Asal radja2 Palembang. Wason Collection, Cornell University, Ithaca, N.Y. (Microfilm.)

Babad Mataram. Manuscript, Wason Collection, Cornell University, Ithaca, N.Y. Vols. I, II, V. (Microfilm.)

Babad Tanah Djawi. Edited by Meinsma. Leiden, 1941.

Balai Poestaka (ed.). *Babad Tanah Djawi.* Djakarta, 1939. Vols. 16, 21.

Basham, A. L. *The Wonder that was India.* London, 1956.

Berg, C. C. "The Islamization of Java," *Studia Islamica*, Vol. IV, 1955.

_____. "Javaansche Geschiedschrijving," in F. W. Stapel, *Geschiedenis van Nederlandsch Indië.* Amsterdam, 1938. Vol. II.

Berg, L. W. C. van den. *De Inlandsche Rangen en Titels.* Batavia, 1887.

Bosch, F. D. K. "C. C. Berg and Ancient Javanese History," *Bijdragen tot de Taal-, Land- en Volkenkunde*, Vol. 112, 1956.

Brandes, J. "Nog iets over een reeds vroeger gepubliceerde Piagem van Sultan Ageng," *Tijdschrift voor Indische Taal-, Land- en Volkenkunde*, Vol. 32, 1889.

Burger, D. H. *Structural Changes in Javanese Society.* Translated by Leslie H. Palmier. Translation Series, Modern Indonesia Project, Cornell University, Ithaca, N.Y., 1956.

Casparis, J. G. de. *Airlangga.* Inaugural speech at Airlangga University. Surabaja, 1958.

Coulborn, Rushton. *Feudalism in History.* Princeton, 1956.

Dewantara, Ki Hadjar. *Beoefening van Letteren en Kunst in het Pakoe Alamsche geslacht.* Jogjakarta, 1931.

Djajadiningrat, Hoesein. *Critische beschouwingen over de Sadjarah Banten.* A dissertation, Haarlem, 1913.

Djajadiningrat I, R. M. H. *Margowirjo*. Surakarta, 1908.

Domis, H. J. *De Residentie Passoeroeang*. The Hague, 1836.

Drewes, G. W. J. *Drie Javaansche Goeroe's*. A dissertation, Leiden, 1925.

_____. *Eenvoudig hedendaagsch Javaansch Proza*. Leiden, 1946.

Duyvendak, J. P. H. *Inleiding tot de Ethnologie van de Indonesische Archipel*. Groningen, 1954.

Faber, G. H. *Er werd een stad geboren*. Surabaja, 1953.

Geertz, Clifford. *The Religion of Java*. Glencoe, I11., 1960.

Gericke, J. F. C. *Javaansch-Nederduitsch Woordenboek*. Amsterdam, 1847.

Gonda, J. *Sanskrit in Indonesia*, Nagpur, 1952.

Graaf, H. J. de. *Geschiedenis van Indonesië*. 's-Gravenhage, 1949.

_____. "Het Kadjoran Vraagstuk," *Djawa*, Vol. 20 (1940), nos. 4-5.

_____. *Over het ontstaan van de Javaanse Rijkskroniek*. Rijksuniversiteit, Leiden, October 19, 1953.

_____. "De Regering van Panembahan Senapati Ingalaga," *Verh. KI*, Vol. XIII, 1954.

_____. "De Regering van Sultan Agung, Vorst van Mataram," *Verh. KI*, Vol. XXIII, 1958.

_____. "De Regering van Sunan Mangku-rat I, Tegal-Wangi, Vorst van Mataram," *Verh. KI*, Vol. XXXIII, 1961.

_____. "Titels en Namen van Javaanse Vorsten en Groten uit de 16e en 17e eeuw," *Bijdragen tot de Taal-, Land-en Volkenkunde*, Vol. 109, 1953.

Groneman, I. *De Garebeg's te Ngajogjakarta*. 's-Gravenhage, 1895.

Groneman, I. *In de Kedaton te Jogjakarta*. Leiden, 1885.

_____. *Uit en Over Midden-Java*. Zutphen, 1891.

Grunebaum, G. E. von. *Islam*. 2nd ed. London, 1961.

Gunning, J. G. H. *Een Javaansch geschrift uit de 16e eeuw*. Leiden, 1881.

_____. *Roorda's pandji-verhalen*. Leiden, 1896.

Haan, F. de. *Priangan*. Batavia, 1910. Vols. I-IV.

Haar, B. ter. *Adat Law in Indonesia*. New York, 1948.

Hall, D. G. E. (ed.). *Historians of Southeast Asia*. London, 1962.

_____. *History of Southeast Asia*. London, 1955.

Hardjowirogo, R. *Sedjarah Wajang Purwa*. Djakarta, 1952.

Heine-Geldern, R. "Conceptions of State and Kingship in Southeast Asia," *The Far Eastern Quarterly*, Vol. 2, November 1942.

Hidding, K. A. H. *Gebruiken en Godsdienst der Soendaneezen.* Batavia, 1930.

Hockett, C. F. *A Course in Modern Linguistics.* New York, 1958.

Hollander, J. J. de (ed.). "Serat Manik Maja," *VBG,* Vol. XXIV, 1852.

Hooykaas, Ch. *Tantri, de Middel-Javaansche Pancatantra-bewerking.* Leiden, 1929.

Hooykaas, Jacoba. "The Rainbow in Ancient Indonesian Religion," *Bijdragen tot de Taal-, Land- en Volkenkunde.* Vol. 112, 1956.

Humme, H. C. *Abiåså.* 's-Gravenhage, 1878.

Inggris. "De Kalang's in Bagelen," *Djawa,* Vol. 1 (1921), no. 1.

Iqbal, Sir Mohammad. *The Reconstruction of Religious Thought in Islam.* Lahore, 1954.

James, William. *The Varieties of Religious Experience.* New York, 1961.

Jansz, P. *Javaansch-Nederlandsch Woordenboek.* Bandoeng, 1906.

Jasadipura, Kyai (ed. Cohen-Stuart), "Serat Bratajuda," *VBG,* Vol. XXVIII, 1860.

Jasadipura, Kyai. *Serat Rama.* Semarang, 1919.

Johns, A. H. "Sufism as a Category in Indonesian Literature and History," *Journal of Southeast Asian History,* Vol. II, July 1961.

Jonge, J. K. J. de. *De Opkomst van het Nederlandsch Gezag in Post Indië (1595-1610).* 's-Gravenhage, 1869. Vol. IV.

Jonker, J. C. G. *Een Oud-Javaansch Wetboek.* A dissertation, Leiden, 1885.

Juynboll, A. W. T. "Kleine Bijdragen over den Islam op Java," *Bijdragen tot de Taal-, Land- en Volkenkunde van Neder-landsch Indië,* Series 4, Vol. VI (30), 1882.

Juynboll, Th. W. *Handleiding tot de kennis van de Moham-medaansche Wet.* Leiden, 1930.

Kat Angelino, A. D. A. de. *Staatkundig beleid en bestuurszorg in Nederlandsch-Indië.* 's-Gravenhage, 1930 . Vol. II.

Kats, J. *Het Javaansche Toneel.* Batavia, 1923. Vol. I.

Knebel, J. "Babad Pasir volgens een Banjoemaasch handschrift met vertaling," *VBG,* Vol. LI, 1900.

Koentjaraningrat. *Some Social-Anthropological Observations on Gotong Rojong Practices in Two Villages of Central Java.* Translated by Claire Holt. Monograph Series, Modern Indonesia Project, Cornell University, Ithaca, N.Y., 1961.

Kraemer, H. "Tapa," *Djawa*, Vol. 4 (1924).

Lasker, Bruno. *Human Bondage in Southeast Asia*. Chapel Hill, 1950.

Lekkerkerker, C. *Land en Volk van Java*. Groningen, 1938.

Leur, J. C. van. *Indonesian Trade and Society*. The Hague, 1955.

Louw, P. J. F. *De Java Oorlog*. Batavia, 1894.

Mangkunegara IV. *Dwidja Isjwara*. Edited by Padmasusastra. Surakarta, 1899.

Mangkunegara VII, K.G.P.A.A. *On the Wayang Kulit (Purwa) and Its Symbolic and Mystical Elements*. Translated by Claire Holt. Southeast Asia Program Data Paper No. 27, Cornell University, Ithaca, N.Y., 1957.

Mechelen, Ch. te. "Drie en Twintig Teksten van Wajang Stukken (Lakon)," *VBG*, Vol. XL, 1879.

_____, (ed.). "Drie Teksten van Toneelstukken uit de Wajang Poerwa," *VBG*, Vol. XLIII, 1882.

Meilink-Roelofsz, M. A. P. *Asian Trade and European Influence*. The Hague, 1962.

Meinsma, J. J. "Eene proklamatie van een Soeltan van Banten," *Bijdragen tot de Taal-, Land- en Volkenkunde van Neder- landsch Indië*, Series 3, Vol. VIII, 1873.

Meyer, D. H. "Over het bendewezen op Java," *Indonesië*, Vol. III, July 1949-May 1950.

Mook, H. J. van. "Kuta Gede," in The Indonesian Town. The Hague, 1958.

Ogburn, William F., and Meyer F. Nimkoff. *A Handbook of Sociology*. London, 1953.

Oudemans, G. J. *Javaansche Wetten*. Jogjakarta, 1897.

Padmasusastra. *Serat Patibasa*. Batavia, 1916.

_____. *Serat Tatatjara*. Semarang, 1911.

Padmosoekotjo, S. *Ngengrengan Kasusastran Djawa*. Jogjakarta, 1958. Vols. I, II.

Pakem Ringgit Poerwa. Weltevreden, 1921. Vols. V, VI.

Paku Buwana IV. *Wulangreh*. Edited by R. M. Soewardi. Kediri, 1929.

Paku Buwana IX. *Serat Wara Isjwara*. Edited by Padmasusastra. Surakarta, 1898.

Pigeaud, Th. G. Th. "Afkondigingen van Soeltans van Banten voor Lampoeng," *Djaw a*, Vol. 9 (1929), nos. 4-5.

_____. "Alexander, Sakèndèr en Sénopati,51 *Djawa*, Vol. 7 (1927), nos. 5-6.

_____. *Javaanse Volksvertoningen*. Batavia, 1938.

_____. *Javaans-Nederlands Handwoordenboek*. Groningen/Batavia, 1938.

_____. *Java in the 14th Century*. The Hague, 1960-1963.
vols. I-V

_____. "K. P. Arja Adipati Danoeredja VII," *Djawa*, Vol. 11 (1931), no. 4.

_____. "De Serat Tjabolang en de Serat Tjentini, Inhoudsopgaven," *VBG*, Vol. LXXII, 2, 1933.

_____. "Vorstenlandsche Garebeg's," *Djawa*, Vol. 12 (1932).

Poensen, C. "Amangkoe Buwana II (Sepoeh)," *Bijdragen tot de Taal-, Land- en Volkenkunde van Nederlandsch Indië*, Vol. 58, 1905.

Poerbatjaraka, R. M. Ng. *Kapustakan Djawi*. Djakarta, 1952.

_____, (ed.). *Nitiçastra*. Translated by R. M. B. Djajahendra. Batavia, 1940.

Pranatjitra. Batavia, 1932.

Prijohoetomo. *Nawaruci*. A dissertation, Groningen, 1934.

Rassers, W. H. *Pañji, the Culture Hero*. The Hague, 1959.

"Reis van den G. G. G. W. Baron van Imhoff in en door de Jakatrasche-Bovenlanden 1744," *Bijdragen tot de Taal-, Land- en Volkenkunde van Nederlandsch Indië*, New Series, Vol. VII, 1864.

Repertorium op de Koloniale Literatuur 1595-1865. Amsterdam, 1877.

Rinkes, D. A. "Babad Tjirebon," *VBG*, Vol. LIX, 1911.

Roorda, T. *Beknopte Javaansche Grammatica*. Zwolle, 1906.

_____. *Javaansch Brievenboek*. Leiden, 1904.

_____. *Javaansch-Nederlandsch Handwoordenboek*. Amsterdam, 1901.

Rosenthal, E. I.J. *Political Thought in Medieval Islam*. Cambridge, 1962.

Rothenbuhler, F. J. "Rapport van den Staat en Gesteldheid van het Landschap Sourabaija," *VBG*, Vol. XLI, 1881.

Rouffaer, G. P. "Vorstenlanden," *Adatrechtbundel*, Vol. XXXIV, serie D, No. 81.

Sara -Samuccaya. New Delhi, 1962.

Sarkar, Benoy Kumar. *Creative India*. Lahore, 1937.

Schrieke, B. *Indonesian Sociological Studies*. The Hague, 1957. Vols. I, II.

Selection of important documents belonging to the Collection Kern and Gobee (in the possession of the Koninklijk Instituut voor Taal-,

Land- en Volkenkunde, Leiden). Wason Collection, Cornell University, Ithaca, N.Y. (Microfilm.)

Selosoemardjan. *Social Changes in Jogjakarta.* Ithaca, 1962.

Serat Padalangan Ringgit Purwa. Batavia, 1932. Vols. XV, XXII.

Serat Pananggalan Djawi. Jogjakarta, 1935.

Serat Tjentini, (ed.)Bataviaasch Genootschap voor Kunsten en Wetenschappen. Batavia, 1912-1915. Vols. I-VIII.

Shorto, H. L. "A Mon Genealogy of Kings," in D. G. E. Hall, *Historians of Southeast Asia.* London, 1962.

Soehari, S. "Pinggir," *Djawa,* Vol. 9 (1929), nos. 3-4-5.

Soemantri Hardjodibroto (trans.). "De Wijzigingen der gebruiken en gewoonten aan het Solosche Hof," *Djawa,* Vol. 11 (1931), no. 4.

Soeripto. *Ontwikkelingsgang der Vorstenlandsche Wetboeken.* A dissertation, Leiden, 1929.

Stutterheim, W. F. "The Meaning of the Hindu-Javanese Candi," *Journal of the American Oriental Society,* Vol. 51, No. 1, March, 1931.

Tarling, Nicholas. *Piracy and Politics in the Malay World.* Melbourne, 1963.

Tjabang Bagian Bahasa Jogjakarta. *Ngungak isining Serat Astabrata.* Jogjakarta, 1958.

Tjan Tjoe Siem. *Hoe Koeroepati zich zijn vrouw verwerft.* Leiden, 1938.

Veth, P. J. *Java.* Haarlem, 1875-1907. Vols. II, III.

Vliet, J. van der. "Pandoe," *Bijdragen tot de Taal-, Land-en Volkenkunde van Nederlandsch Indië,* Series 4, Vol. III (27), 1879.

Vollenhoven, C. van. *Het Adatrecht van Nederlandsch Indië.* Leiden, 1918.

_____. *Javaansch Adatrecht.* Leiden, 1923.

Wedyodipoero. "Het Wajangspel," in *Congres voor Javaansche Cultuur Ontwikkeling.* Surakarta, 1918.

Wertheim, W. F. *Indonesian Society in Transition.* The Hague, 1956.

Winter, C. F. "Regtspleging over de onderdanen van Z. H. den Soesoehoenan van Soerakarta," *Tijdschrift voor Neër-landsch Indië.* Batavia, 1844.

Winter, C. F., Senior. *Javaansche Zamenspraken.* Amsterdam, 1862.

Wiselius, J. A. B. "Djaja Baja," *Bijdragen tot de Taal-, Land- en Volkenkunde van Nederlandsch Indië,* Series 3, Vol. VII (19), 1872.

Wulfften Palthe, P. M. van. *Over het bendewezen op Java.* Amsterdam,

1948.

Zimmer, Heinrich. *Myths and Symbols in Indian Art and Civilization.* New York, 1962.

Zoetmulder, P. J. *Pantheisme en Monisme in de Javaansche Soeloek-litteratuur.* A dissertation, Nijmegen, 1935.

A STANDARD PIJAGEM OF BEKEL-SHIP

Text

Pijagem. Iki lajangku pratanda pijagem, Kyai Ngabei Anu, abdidalem Anu ing Surakarta, katjekela marang Anu ing desa Anu.

Mulane njekel lajangku pratanda pijagem, dene takdadekake bekel ing desa Anu gawening wong loro utawa sakikil:

* satabon padukuhane, sabandjar pakarangane, sapadas perenge, salebak wukire, den sanggaa padjeg ing dalem satahun 8 rejal anelung puluh wang, urip:

* radja pundut taker tedaking nagara, sarta padjang pasisiran tuwin watesan, apa dene bahu suku, lumebu Garebeg ping telu satahun, sarta jen aku duwe gawe, apa dene dandan-dandan, sarta lumadi: wang krig adji, walan, pamalem, pamulud lan panjumpleng, pasangon putra.

  Lan maneh enggone Anu dadi bekel ngiras tebas, kehing duwit panebas: 100 rupijah, mulih dadi: 250 rupijah, sumurup 10 tahun 20 pasokan pundut, wiwit pasokane ing Bakda Garebeg Mulud tahun Alip angka…tutug pasokane ing Bakda Garebeg Pasa tahun Dje angka… pundut, Mulude Dal bandjur tapak bajar padjeg sabandjure, sadjrone bumi ana ing tebasan, aku nglilakake panguwasa:

* kadjenanga kaebora, kaparokna kairasa, sadedak merange, sa-amis batjine, nandur sarta motjota bekel pamburi. aku wis lila atas wewenange Anu, sanadyan an aa:

* gedang pupus tjinde, djamur tuwuh ing waton, krambil tapas limar, atas dadi duweke Anu, wis mari dadi melikku, kosok-baline menawa ana srilara radjapati,

* getih tjinelung, balung tjinandi,
  aku wis ora njumurupi, tinemua marang Anu dewe.

Djandji sapisan.

Anu ora kena ngrusak desa, ambubarake wong tjilik kang awit saka parentah sija-nganiaja, negor kitri isih ana nipkahe, sanadyan negor kaju tahun kang dadi wawajanganing desa, ija ora kena.

Djandji pindo.

Anu ora kena ngubungi laku palatjidra kandeg kampiran wong ala, menawa anu nerak papatjak iki, sanadyan bumi durung pundut, amesti tak dedel tanpa prakara sarta kowe tak potjot saka kabe kelanmu.

Patjuwan-patjuwan marang wong tjilik ing desa Anu, gede-tjilik, tuwa-anom, lanang-wadon, pada manut mituruta apa barang parentahe Anu kang bener betjik.

Taha jen tan angestokna, atanapi jen maidoa, amesti kaplaksana ing Parentah.

Surakarta kaping…

(from: Padmasusastra, Serat Patibasa, Batavia, 1916, p. 325)

* Note the custom-coined, stereotyped expressions.

Translation

Decree of Institution. This is a letter of mine, Kyai Ngabei So and So (title and name of lessor) in the King's service as Such and Such (rank of lessor) in Surakarta, as a token of institution, to be held by So and So (name of lessee) of the village of Such and Such (habitat of lessee).

The reason for receiving this decree of mine is that I make him *bekel* in the village of Such and Such, having jurisdiction over two persons (meaning: *tjatjah*) or otherwise named *sakikil*:
with all surrounding barren lands (*tabon*) and hamlets (*padukuhan*), including its orchards and gardens (*bandjar pekarangan*), its rocks (*padas*) and slopes (*pereng*), its in-entures (*lebak*: valley) and hills (*wukir*), with the duty of paying tax, per year eight *rejal* (1 rejal: 2 guilders) and thirty *wang* (1 wang: 8.5 guilder's cents), plus: the King's own exactions (*radja pundut*) and side-taxes (*taker tedaking nagara*), special *bekel*-services (namely towards his *lurah*: *padjang pasisiran*) and term-money (? *wate-san*), also labor-service (*bahu suku*: lit. shoulder and leg), to be delivered

at the time of the *Garebeg*-feasts three times a year, also whenever I give a fete, or have something to repair, further to provide: money to buy off labor-service for the King (*wang krig adji*), gifts of edibles to the *lurah* (*walan*), contributions tor the Pasa- and Mulud-feasts (*pamalem* and *pamulud*), house-tax (*panjumpleng*) and contributions for the wedding-gift for the Lord's daughters (*pasangon putra*).

Furthermore, the fact of So and So becoming *bekel* also involves an advance payment [of the land-tax] amounting to a hundred guilders, which will be paid back two hundred and fifty guilders, corresponding to 10 years or 20 deliveries [of land-tax], beginning with the first term on the Mulud festivities (Rabi'ulawal 12) of the Alip-year of …and ending with the term on the Pasa festivities [after the Rama-dhan fast] of the Dje-year of…, so that, on the following Mulud of the Dal-year, he must begin again to bring in taxes regularly. As long as the land is still weighted with the advance-payment, I herewith declare I am willing to give consent to the holder of this decree: to knead the clay [for bricks] and wash the sand [for possible gold]; to lease the land out in crop-shares, or to till it on his own, with all its produce be it plant or fish; to install and depose *bekels* of the second grade, [To all these rights] I will not lay claim, even if he should find a banana-tree with leaf-shoots of *tjinde*-silk, mushrooms growing on stone, a coconut-tree with leaf-foils of *limar*-silk [all this symbolizing possible buried treasures], those will all be his property, and will cease being mine. On the other hand if there ever happens to occur: molestation or murder; blood in a pot or bones immured [both indicating mysterious crimes]; I will take my hands off it and the responsibility will all be So and So's.

First clause.

So and So is not allowed to do mishap to the village, to cause flight of the small man because of oppression and misrule, to cut down fruit-bearing trees which still serve as somebody's living; also to cut down trees benefiting the village is not allowed.

Second clause.

So and So is not allowed to involve himself in misconduct; to shelter or give temporary refuge to men of crime; if So and So ever violates these prohibitions, the land I will instantly take back, even if the time agreed upon has not yet expired, and I will depose him from his *bekel*-ship without honor.

Prohibitions to the people of village Such and Such, the big and the small, the young and the old, men as well as women: be obedient to all just and good orders of So and So, and if ever one of you disobeys, or worse still is recalcitrant, that one will be punished, as a warning, by the State. [More usual is that misfortune and unhappiness will befall him].

Surakarta,…(date of issue)…

THE SYSTEMS OF TAXATION AND LABOR LEVY IN LATER MATARAM

Tax and Taxation

It is rather difficult to speak of "state financing" in the modern sense during the second Mataram period, if we understand it as a systematized and overall effort to organize the incomes and expenditures of the state as a whole. This is not only because of the non-existence of a centralized treasury but also because of the incidental way by which financial needs of the state were met. It would be better, then, to speak of the acquisition and distribution of wealth by the state in order to avoid limitations imposed by the use of the modern term.

If we bear in mind the simplicity of state organization in those feudal times, it becomes quite obvious that the meeting of contingent expenditures with contingent exactions as the basis of meeting material and later financial needs must be the most logical consequence of such a principle of simplicity. In other words, during these centuries of royal reign in Mataram, the fullest extent of self-support or "autonomy" was practiced. Virtually every need — grass for the royal steeds, repair of roads, an official's living, a transport department — every one of these was allotted a source of income of its own, a piece of land, a special tax or the manpower of a certain village, with which it had to try to cover all possible, and sometimes quite impossible, expenses. The maintenance of a department, office or institution was left wholly to the ability and moral considerations of the office-holder, a fact quite in harmony with a state organization in which personal authority played such a dominating role.

The court had its own resources for each of its various needs: special districts to provide the rice for the king's table, certain villages to provide coconut-oil, special forests to provide teak-wood for the palace buildings. There was central distribution but only for those members of the king's household who had not received a piece of land for their living; this of course is also applicable on a lesser scale to the vassal's household. There might have been a considerable number of such people,since in the royal household there were hundreds of servants, ranging from those who did simple menial work — sweepers of the many meticulously clean courtyards, carriers of water, and the like — to craftsmen who made the finest works of art and writers of copies with their beautifully ornamented handwriting. In this group must be included the various units of palace guards and crack troops with grandiloquent names. All these workers drew their living directly from the king's treasuries in the form of a regular *tjadong* (portion, ration) of rice and other daily necessities, plus from time to time a *paringan* (gift) of clothing. But even in the king's household, there were several lower offices which were connected to certain specified emoluments, seemingly following a quite ancient custom. For instance, the master craftsmen of the court and also their colleague the *lurah tledek* (master of the public female dancers) had the right to exact contributions from all other people drawing their living from the same trade.[1]

Another fact to take into consideration is that, in a state whose economy is based on entirely autonomous agrarian *desa*-units and whose system of administration is comprised of entirely self-supporting units, a very large part of the exactions from the people, whether in the form of material wealth or manual labor, must necessarily come to the benefit of the holders of power, the king and his vassals. This is especially so when commerce and trade, on which various kinds of duties can be imposed, are thriving. Thus, one can imagine that the accumulation of wealth in the Later Mataram king's treasuries was indeed great. Mataram's direct and frequent interference in the appointment of the chiefs of coastal districts such as Demak, Djepara and Semarang (so unlike its treatment of other vassalages) and the detailed official stipulations concerning harbor cities must be seen in connection with the material benefits accruing from these areas. Some potentates deemed it necessary to enforce the payment

---

1 See also: Pigeaud, *Java in the 14th Century*, Vol. IV, pp. 423, 476.

of duties by sending out armed brigades to patrol the coastal waters for passing merchantmen.[2]

The harbor cities were not alone in being considered important; in inland trade, the numerous small and large market places (called *pasar*) and the all too numerous stops on roads and rivers formed a considerable source of income. A provision in a Javanese legal code, the *Angger Ageng* (the Great Code), mentioned the duty of the people to mount guard over every *pasar* and *bandar* (toll stop) each night,[3] notably to secure the safety of the goods gathered at those places. The Javanese have a special word for the exactions on trade goods, *beja*, which distinguishes them from regular taxes, *padjeg*. The word *beja* originally meant "cost" or "expenditure" in general and it is difficult to discover when it assumed the particular meaning of "duty" or "customs," but the fact that there are places in many coastal towns bearing the name *pabejan* points to a long established practice.[4] These places were also called *pambandaran*.

It may perhaps be of some interest, in connection with the sources of wealth of the State, to see how the Javanese divided the population into four categories according to their usefulness to the state. A *piwulang* written at the beginning of this century states:

lan ana patang prakara, kagunganing kang pradjadi, pradjurit lawan pandita, tri sudagar tjatur tani

and there are four matters forming the properties of the Great Realm (the state), the soldier and the sage, third the merchant and fourth the peasant.

An explanation is added:

the soldier is the fortress of the king, the peasant the food of the state, the merchant the clothing of the land and the sage provides the benefaction of prayers.[5]

---

2 See further: M. A. P. Meilink-Roeloefsz, *Asian Trade and European Influence*, The Hague, 1962, Ch. III and V (Part 4). Also: Tarling, *op. cit.*, p. 189.

3 Oudemans, *op. cit.*, p. 36, "Angger Ageng," art. 23.

4 In Surabaya a regular market, now three miles from the river mouth, is named *pabejan*.

5 R. M. H. Djajadiningrat I, *op. cit.*, p. 115.

It is quite apparent from this *piwulang* that, while the peasantry must provide the food needed, the riches of the state had to be extracted mainly from trade and commerce, for the word "clothing" (*busana*) includes all wearing apparel, particularly ornaments and jewelry. Duties imposed on trade ranged from three to six percent differing according to the particular port through which the goods entered or according to the country of origin, but about four percent seems to have been the common rate. For the Javanese ports, Tomé Pires' account (1512) mentioned the figure four as duty.[6] In addition to the duties, most potentates demanded the customary gifts or presents. The inland trade, up the rivers or along the few main roads, probably suffered a heavier burden of taxes, not because of higher rates, but because of the great number of toll houses set up by the king or his vassals. The situation became the more stifling to trade when toll stops were let out to wealthy natives and foreigners, notably Chinese, and extortion and over-charging was practiced to an immoderate degree. Schrieke mentioned an example from the year 1787.[7] In 1824, this evil had become so common that whole territories, for instance both the regencies of Madiun and Magetan, were leased for their toll gates to a single Chinese,who subsequently divided the region into smaller districts to sell; the lesser lease-holders subdivided again and farmed out still smaller parts of their districts to the "highest bidder, or to put it clearly, to the most unscrupulous Chinese." Thus, each piece of goods passing through such a regency was officially burdened by the regular toll plus three times a third of the sum and unofficially it might be very much more, for every leaseholder had the right to keep a third of the tax imposed for his own benefit.[8]

The acquisition of great masses of riches which tolls and duties made possible notwithstanding, the kingdom relied for its orderly functioning as an institutional organization first and foremost on the peasantry, whose labor provided the means necessary not only to till the soil but also to do the work of maintaining and sustaining the state, from road repairs to transporting goods, from serving in a nobleman's retinue to fighting in the king's army. Having control over a populous territory was therefore

---

6   Meilink-Roeloefsz, *op. cit.*, p. 113.
7   Schrieke, *op. cit.*, Vol. II, p. 115.
8   Louw, *op. cit.*, p. 12.

considered of great advantage and a lessening of population through evacuation was anxiously guarded against.[9]

In connection with the importance attached to the density of population, we must introduce here the term *tjatjah*, a word used to denote measurement of territories in terms of taxable land. The word itself meant in ancient Java a notch or indentation carved on a stick or a *papan* (board) to facilitate counting; eventually it took on the special meaning of "number" as well. At the end of the last century, Dutch writers, notably Rothenbuhler, Rouffaer and later van Vollen-hoven,[10] defined *tjatjah* as the unit of arable land which produces enough for one farming family to live on, a term usually equated with the word *karja* which originally meant work or task, and with the word *bahu*, originally meaning arm or upper-arm. Truly, both of the latter words denote work, here ostensibly the amount of work to be done to till the soil. Modern standardization puts four *bahus* into one *djung*, approximately 28,386 square meters.

A possible explanation of the change in meaning of the word *tjatjah* from number to unit of land might be arrived at if we take into account the traditional classification of the members of the *desa* community according to their rights and duties toward the *desa*. Up to the present time, the inhabitants of a *desa* are divided into four categories:

1. the *kuli kentjeng* or *kuli ngarep*, *kuli kuwat*, *kuli gogol*, *kuli sikep*, the full-fledged member of the *desa* community who has received his traditional share of the communal lands of the *desa*;
2. the *kuli kendo* or *kuli mburi*, *kuli setengah kentjeng*, who owns both a yard and a house on it and who is on the waiting-list for vacancies in the ranks of the shareholders;
3. the *tumpang* or *indung* or *pondok karang*, who owns only a house located in another man's yard;
4. the *tumpang tlosor* or *pondok slosor*, who does not even own a house but boards with another family.

---

9 See pages 67, 76.
10 Schrieke, *op. cit.*, Vol. II, p. 158; Rouffaer, *op. cit.*, p. 71 ; Rothenbuhler, *op. cit.*, p. 34; C. van Vollenhoven, *Het Adatrecht van Nederlandsch Indië*, Leiden, 1918, p. 551.

Much has been written about this system of categorization by noted authorities like van Vollenhoven[11] and more recently by the anthropologist Koentjaraningrat[12] in his research on the practice of *gotong-rojong* (system of mutual help) which has explained much about the responsibilities of the villager vis-a-vis his community. It therefore suffices to note here that the first category of members or "kerndorpers" (core villager), using Professor van Vollenhoven's term, has the largest share of duties, *gawe desa*, towards the community: the core villagers must pay taxes, work in the field of the village chief or other notables or accompany them in their retinue (*pantjen* service); they also must maintain irrigation ditches, appear on *gugur-gunung*, stand guard duty (*djaga*) at night and, formerly, they had to serve in the armies of the lord. The next three categories of villagers have decreasing shares of the *gawe desa* so that the last group, for instance, is only required to appear when all members of the village, except children and the aged, are called out to do the annual cleaning of the cemetery or to help overcome a serious mishap affecting the whole village. This is what is indicated by the word *gugur-gunung* or *kerigan*. Outside the *desa*, in state service, *gugur-gunung* was a general call to the whole population to come out in times of natural calamities or in case of war but also to do special, extra-ordinary work like the building of a palace, and no doubt, in former times, the building of temples.

The importance of the distinctions among members of the village community lies in the stress customary law put on the first category of villagers, the *kuli kentjeng* or *kuli kuwat* and this is immediately apparent because *kentjeng* (taut, tight) and *kuwat* (strong, able-bodied) both denote strength and ability. IT is they who have the strength to carry the burden of taxation and labor-levy for they have the means to pay taxes, namely their share in the communal land. The principal tax, the *padjeg* or *padjeg bumi* (land tax) is also called *padjeg sikep* or *sikep* tax, and the shareholder of communal land was and is still called *kuli sikep*. This perhaps means that only this first category of villagers originally was burdened with the land tax. It is therefore most probable that the word *tjatjah* formerly denoted

11 Van Vollenhoven, *Javaansch Adatrecht*, p. 20ff.

12 Koentjaraningrat, *Some Social-Anthropological Observations on Gotong Rojong Practices in Two Villages of Central Java*, trans. Claire Holt, Monograph Series, Modern Indonesia" Project, Cornell University, Ithaca, N.Y. 1961.

the number of these shareholders in a certain district rather than the total area of arable land. At any rate, the exact amount of arable land was rather difficult to determine in Old Java, judging from the difficulties Raffles encountered in his efforts to realize a system of cadastral registration. When later on the convenience of more modern precision and exactness was sought, *tjatjah* came to denote and be identified with the *bahu* as a measurement of land. The fact that some territories mentioned in Schrieke's book were measured for different *tjatjah*-counts at different times strengthens the suspicion that the *tjatjah*-number referred only to the amount of tax that the ruler expected to draw from a territory given in appanage; how that amount was to be gathered was entirely the concern of the appanage-holder. But here, too, tradition formed a powerful check, for most of the regions were indicated rather constantly with the same *tjatjah*-numbers.[13] The following are some regions with their *tjatjah*-numbers as they appear in Schrieke's book:

Lowanu	100 *tjatjah*					350	(in 1813)
(as listed *in Pustaka Radja Purwa*)							
Panaraga		12,000	(1678)	12,000	(1709)	12,000	(1773)
Kadiri	5,000			4,000	"	8,500	"
Patjitan	500			2,000	"	400	"
Kertasana	3,000	3,000	"	3,000	"	3,000	"
						850	(1826)

Two other points must also be mentioned in this connection. First, recent research in the villages of East Java has shown that the communal land has been divided into permanent shares (*tjaton*) exactly equal in terms of productivity so that less fertile lands have been divided into slightly larger shares. The latter are usually the lands situated "at the back," that is, at the furthest points from the irrigation ditch. When the land is divided into shares of equal size, the inequality of production is neutralized by the practice of yearly rotation of shares, so that the *gogol ngarep*, the "front"-shareholders with the most fertile lands along the irrigation ditch, will

13 Schrieke, *op. cit.*, Vol. II, p. 183.

eventually become the *gogol-buri* with shares at the "back." This system is called *glebagan* (turnover).

Secondly, it is important to include here some discussion of units of measurements. According to sources consulted, the number of *bahus* going into one *djung* was 2 (Peka-longan and Surabaya) or 4 and 4½ (Middle Java),4 being the usual figure. Rothenbuhler also defines other units of measure. One *Jonk* (*djung*) was equal to 5600 Javanese square *ru* (yard). One *ru* was equal to 8½, 9, 9½, 10 or 10½ Rhynland yards. The Javanese word *ru* is taken from the Dutch *roe, roede* (yard).[14] Since the number of shareholders in the *desas* was constant — although the shares differed slightly in size — and the definition of *bahus* was not constant — that is, it differed from area to area — our conclusion is perhaps justified that originally the *tjatjah* referred to the number of shareholders of communal land in a certain district. This is the more probable if we observe that in principle all other land was exempted — at first — from tax. This included dry land (*tegalan*), free-villages (*perdikan*), the king's domain (*narawita*), and lands given as "wages" to village notables (*lungguh, bengkok*).

After this brief discussion of the unit of enumeration for the purpose of taxation, we may proceed now to the problem of the taxes themselves. In order to gain a clearer understanding of the Javanese tax system, we ought to consider first the traditional way of sharing gains accruing from services rendered. Mutual rendering of services proves to be a very old practice especially in a simple agrarian community where continuous care was needed to attend to the wet-rice fields and where payment for labor in money was rare. It was and to a certain extent is still usual that rice-fields are tilled, weeded, the small dikes along the fields maintained, and later the grain harvested within a system of mutual help. However, the labor "sharers" also acquire rights the realization of which they insist upon very keenly, namely the right to help with the harvesting and to 10-ceive a certain part of what is gathered; the share differs according to the amount of labor contributed in the tilling of the soil and the care of the crop. In the region of East Java up to the present time, the custom is as follows. A co-worker who helps (a) with the tilling, weeding, dike-maintaining and harvesting receives one third of the rice his family (wife, daughters) can

---

14 Van Vollenhoven, *Javaansch Adatrecht*, p. 46; Rothenbuhler, *op . cit.*, p. 27.

harvest; (b) with the weeding, dike-maintenance, harvesting receives one fourth; (c) with the weeding and harvesting only receives one fifth; and (d) with the harvesting only — this when a field is harvested in a "come-one-come-all" (*krotjokan*) — receives one sixth. The share for services rendered is called *bawon* or — especially in East Java — *sasrahan*. It must be noted that digging the soil and dike-maintenance are done by men, weeding and harvesting by the womenfolk, and also that the grain is harvested ear by ear, so that the amount that one person can gather is very limited. If we take into account the fact that the *maron*-system (half for the owner and half for the tiller of a piece of land) is also quite old, we may then come to the conclusion that the five-part division of the produce of village land — one-fifth to the village authorities, two-fifths to the king, two-fifths to the peasant tiller-shareholder — mentioned in Rouffaer's invaluable report,[15] could be based or at least modeled on these age-old customs in the *desas*. That is to say, in principle, the land belongs to the *desa*, and the king like the village notables receives his share for services rendered (protection and administration). Indeed there have been no examples found where the king took away village land in such a way that the villager was entirely deprived of his traditional share of the produce of the land, except of course when land was confiscated for purposes other than for farmland.

The two-fifths share of the king — in actuality half of the produce of the land tilled by the peasants after one fifth was set apart for the *desa* notables — was called *padjeg, padjeg-sikep* or *padjeg bumi*, which formed the principal tax. Later developments led to standardization so that the tax was fixed at 1 *Real* [fl. 3.00 (Dutch) or approximately $3.00 (U.S.)] per 1 *djung* or ¼ *real* for 1 *bahu*. According to Rouffaer around 1755 the tax was raised so that every *bahu* then had to yield 1 *real* a year in tax.[16] For the outer provinces, the *mantjanegara*, where governors managed the territories, the king received a lesser share. Rouffaer reconstructs it as follows: one-fifth for the village notables, two-fifths to the peasant shareholder, one-fifth of the sovereign's two-fifth part (or 2/25 of the whole produce) to the provincial governor (*bupati*), still another 2/25 to the

15 Rouffaer, *op. cit.*, pp. 68, 69. See also Adam, *op. cit.*, p. 331.
16 Rouffaer, *op. cit.*, p. 71.

governor's officers as a whole, and the rest or 6/25 to the king himself, or in percentages subsequently 20%, 40%, 8%, 8%, and 24%.[17] The governor's share, as well as those of his officials and of the village notables,were of course given not in produce but in areas of land. Moreover, it was quite possible for the king to add some lands to the territory of a favorite governor,[18] and appropriation of another vassal's rights by annexation of land was not impossible.

In the core regions where the sovereign had granted the right to extract taxes to an appanage-holder, one-fifth of the land was set apart for the *bekels* who actually administered for their *lurah* or *patuh* (master), the appanage-holder, performing police duties but mainly collecting taxes.[19] The *bekel* received from his master a *piagem*, a certificate of installment, the form of which was traditional and thus uniform and helps the student acquire a better understanding of situations and conditions of the time.[20] *Piagems*, at least those that have been preserved which date from the eighteenth and nineteenth centuries, almost invariably reveal a practice which became widespread at the time, namely the farming out of the tax-gathering privilege to financiers who had advanced money to the appanage-holder; these financiers were Javanese and not infrequently foreigners, Dutch or Chinese. Strangely enough, because the right to gather taxes was given to the creditor he was constituted a *bekel* as well. A *piagem* of 1825 mentions a *bekel pamadjegan Tjina*, a Chinese tax-*bekel*.[21] To what extent they might exercise the *bekel* rights other than tax-collecting cannot yet be determined, but a story from about 1850 of a Chinese woman who continued to exercise the rights of her late husband as a *bekel Tjina* seems to indicate that these rights were far-reaching, including appointing and deposing the lesser officials, *demangs* and lesser-*bekels* in their districts.[22] These practices might indicate, however, that the sale or lease of land by the sovereign was not thought to be permissible and the king's or officers' need for cash was usually met by farming out the right to collect taxes —

---

17 *Ibid.*, p. 73.
18 *Babad Tanah Djawi*, p. 193.
19 See also p. 118.
20 See Appendix I.
21 Roorda, *Brievenboek*, p. 10.
22 T. Roorda, *Beknopte Javaansche Grammatica*, Zwolle, 1906, p. 250ff. This book was written in 1874.

essentially the right of usufruct — to the highest bidder. But again, the fact was that the right of tax-collection might be farmed out for a very long or even an unlimited span of time. Even when, later, land-lease (only to Europeans) was made possible in the "Vorstenlanden" to meet the demands of European sugar and tobacco plantations, the lessee acquired public rights as well; namely, he was permitted to requisition labor from the people,[23] a true trait of the old appanage system. This system lasted until 1918. That these practices to a great extent corrupted the purity of the appanage system can easily be seen.

A fact that has always attracted the attention of the superficial observer of Javanese feudal society is the seemingly endless number of exactions which the king's government could extract from the people; the picture of the Javanese peasant heavily burdened with taxes is a common one. There were indeed many kinds of taxes. Rothenbuhler's report listed twenty-five.[24] Another record dated Semarang, August 21. 1830, arrived at the impressive number of thirty-seven.[25]

They ranged from a tax on the produce of the land to simple fees, from exactions to meet expenses connected with the sending of envoys and the reception of important guests to a contribution given to the superintendent of water in the *desa*, from obligatory delivery of chickens and ducks to the lord's kitchen to payments to the district chief adjudicating a dispute between villages, from fees for weddings, divorces, dividing an inheritance, and holding a theatrical performance to contributions of a religious character. One can see that taxes had a great variety of objectives and purposes, many of which cannot be regarded as belonging strictly within the scope of taxation. However, taxation did not affect all classes of the population and not all taxes were collected regularly. Furthermore, the Javanese themselves seem to make a distinction between the principal tax, the *padjeg*, and all other exactions or contributions to the state (the king), the *taker turun*[26] or *pundutan*. The policy of *ad hoc* or contingent financing forced the state to create for any expenditure, however small it

---

23 A. D. A. de Kat Angelino, *Staatkundig beleid en bestuurs-zorg in Nederlandsch Indië*, 's-Gravenhage, 1930, Vol. IT, p. 532.
24 Rothenbuhler, *op. cit.*, p. 35ff.
25 *Selection...Collection Kern and Gobee*, no. 28. See also: van Vollenhoven, *Javaansch Adatrecht*, p. 44.
26 Van Vollenhoven, *Javaansch Adatrecht*, p. 44. Also Rouffaer, *op. cit.*, p. 87.

might be, its own special source of income which most likely would be in the form of contributions. All this should prove that the usual assumption that the feudal population was heavily burdened by taxation is inaccurate, for the burden was sporadically,not consistently, heavy.

The Use of Labor

The importance of exactions in the form of produce and later money for the financing of the state could not match the importance to the functioning of the state of exactions in the form of the manual labor of the people. The lack of labor-saving implements and especially the relative smallness of the peasant's landholding made man's raw physical strength or, in more modern terms, unskilled labor the only possible means of production and so of wealth. Labor came, then, to be identified with the small man, the common villager with his simple and rather "backward" demands, from whom traditionally labor-service was extracted. Any exemption from these levies was considered a special favor, and indeed this was the first and foremost privilege of the man in the king's service of almost any rank, down to all members of the village administration. The officials had, in fact, to appear at work parties but — and this was the great difference — as the leaders, overseers, and not as workers. All Javanese agreed that only on the battlefield must the leader really participate, for there he had to be the spearhead of his troops.

But the implication that the Javanese must consider manual labor degrading is a very misleading one because every Javanese from whatever class at least once in his life, in his youth and during any apprenticeship for a job, had to endure the most humble servitude. This period formed a most important part of his education, teaching him self-restraint and so the concept of *tepa slira*, and gave him a sure and reliable standard — because of personal experience — when later as a leader he would demand work from subordinates.[27]

Bearing in mind the diversity of taxes, fees and contributions, we might expect that the list of labor-services to be rendered to the state must also be long. Roughly classified, there were two types of labor-service, the work

---

27 See page 95.

to be done for the village (*gawe desa*) and the work to be done for the state and so the king (*gawe adji*). The services could also be classified as general or public service — which included watch-duties, repair and maintenance of roads, dikes, waterworks, bridges and the like — and personal service rendered to dignitaries for their personal benefit (*pantjen*) — working in their fields, repairing their houses or accompanying them to court to take care of their steeds, to be their bodyguards or to carry their luggage. Later, providing manpower for the transport along the main roads of goods (*pikulan*) and persons (*tandon*) became a burdensome duty. It was done in relays by the people of *desas* along the road. Military service was of course a primary duty, although the common villager usually served only as bearers of food and other necessities for the troops. Almost always these men, or their fellow villagers for them, had to provide their own food when serving away from home. Again, the burden of labor exactions fell entirely upon the shoulders of the villager-shareholder of communal land, the *kuli kentjeng* mentioned above. It was therefore not surprising that in times of oppression the only way to free oneself from the burden of tax and labor-levy was to leave the land, which actually meant that one discarded the status of *kuli kentjeng*. It must be noted, however, that,with the introduction of the "culture system" by the Dutch, the duty to serve in compulsory labor gangs seemingly was extended to include all house owners.[28]

Rothenbuhler's estimates from the beginning of the nineteenth century, although given only for the district of Sura-baja, will be of some use here for they give an impression of the amount of labor extracted from the whole people.[29] From each village six to seven men a day would be assigned as follows: two to render personal services to dignitaries; one to dispatch instructions and other official news; one to cut grass for the horses of the *Djajengsekar* (an old, native police corps recognized by the Dutch); one to work on the construction of a public building; one to serve as a carrier for the transport of goods; and one to work in the government coffee plantation. Every village was assigned its share according to its distance from the work presently to be done. A regulation of 1887

---

28 Rothenbuhler, *op. cit.*, p. 44.
29 *Ibid.*, pp. 46, 47.

mentions the *bau paneman* ("workers of six"), namely *kuli kentjengs* of
desas in the mountainous Gunung Kidul district (South Mataram) who
were required to work in the forests every six days for a day, cutting down
and transporting the valuable teak-wood.[30] Daendels had laid down
directives as to how many men Javanese chiefs might be alotted: for a
bupati, 170 men a day not including musicians, *topeng* (mask) dancers
and *wajang* dancers; for a *patih*, one-fourth of that number; for principal
mantris and *djeksas* and the close relatives of the *bupati*, one-eighth; lesser
mantris, one-sixteenth; lower officials, one man per day. Rothenbuhler
gave the number of 5000 men a day in the service of government and
officials, and the total number of the population of the two Surabaja
regencies as 143,662 excluding the families of the two *bupatis*. People had
to work in total four or five months a year in levy-service and from six to
seven months where government plantations were located.

An account of labor-exaction in the kingdom of Later Mataram would
obviously not be complete without mentioning the special classes of
people who, because of their low social status, were destined to do heavy
and toilsome — and so to other people undignified — labor, notably
slaves, convicts and the three groups of people called the Kalang, Gadjah
and Pinggir.

To say that slavery did not exist in feudal Mataram is untrue. An old
Javanese code of law mentions four ways by which a free man could become
a slave (*kawula*) : as a prisoner of war, because of an unpaid fine, because
of "leaving his master's (*gusti*) house" — this perhaps means escape —
and because one "enslaves himself because of food," which means that
a man might voluntarily become a slave to secure himself a living and
protection. With her husband's consent, a wife could sell herself into
slavery.[31] A proclamation of Sultan Zainul Abidin of Banten stipulated
that someone guilty of robbery or piracy was to be killed and his wife and
children were to be taken to the king's palace "to become his slaves." It was
dated 1690.[32] So slavery must have existed too in Later Mataram. However,

---

30 Oudemans, *op. cit.*, under "Pranatan Kabupaten Gunung Kidul," art. 5.

31 Jonker, *op. cit.*, arts. 169, 171.

32 Th. Pigeaud, "Afkondigingen van Soeltans van Banten voor Lampoeng," *Djawa*, Vol. 9
   (1929), nos. 4-5. See for further references on slavery, *Repertorium op de Koloniale Literatuur
   1595-1865*, Amsterdam, 1877, Vol. I, under Nos. 5661, 5665, 5671, 5672, 5677, 5681.

a more important question in connection with the use of manpower by the state is whether slave labor was used *en masse* and intensively so that it became a real economic asset. It is doubtful that it was, for the state or its dignitaries had easy access to manual labor through the labor-levy, as we have seen above. Wertheim is also of the opinion that generally speaking the burden of slavery in Java was a mild one,[33] which is quite in accord with the attitude of familial protectiveness which formed a marked characteristic of social communication throughout Java. Moreover, when referring to another kind of slave, Javanese literature uses the word *batur tukon* or "bought servants." Perhaps it was sensed that there must be some difference between the traditional, custom-regulated concept of *kawula* and the more economically determined *batur tukon*, perhaps referring to those who later were brought in through foreign sea trade.[34] Further work is needed to define clearly the meaning of both terms.

In connection with the use of the two other categories of suppliers of manpower, the convicts and the three named groups, we must mention a most provocative work dealing with the early development of the town of Surabaja in which the writer, Faber, very ingeniously — and this is the exact word to describe his efforts — has tried to give a plausible explanation for forced labor by convicts and other undesirable persons.[35] In former times, the king decreed that some regions spread throughout Java were places for deportees. Perhaps it is likely that these places were chosen for this purpose because they were *angker*, having the reputation of being the dwelling-places of eery ghosts and evil spirits, for they were mostly barren hills, dark jungles or swampy coasts, avoided by man because of their ill reputations. Indeed, even now the Lodaja region of South Blitar in East Java is believed to be the habitat of the were-tigers (*matjan-gadungan*), and it had been for a long time a place of exile or princes who had wronged against the king. Apart from the politically undesirable persons, convicts, adulterers and other criminals, persons suffering from hideous diseases like lepers, frambesia victims, and also

---

33 W. F. Wertheim, *Indonesian Society in Transition*, The Hague, 1956, p. 230.

34 The *Babad Tanah Djawi* mentioned "servants bought-men" of a Balinese merchant of Gresik who fought with the troops of Adipati Djajengrana of Surabaja against Mataram. (*Babad Tanah Djawi*, p. 310). Also mentioned were the "bought men" of the Adipati of Tuban. It is to be noted that these two towns were harbors of international trade.

35 G. H. von Faber, *Er werd een stad geboren*, Surabaja, 1953.

cretins, albinos, the deformed and others who bore the stamp of evil were usually deported with their families; the last category of undesirables were to be accompanied by their mothers.[36] The exiles were expelled for as long as they lived. The story of the legendary spirit-queen Lara Kidul, ruler of the Indian Ocean, seems to confirm the stories about the existence of such a colony of untouchables along the southern coast of Mataram. The queen was formerly a beautiful princess who, suffering from a horrible and incurable disease of the skin, committed suicide by flinging herself from the high cliffs of the south coast into the mighty waves. The sea restored her beauty and made her queen. The curative power of sea water for skin diseases might be another *raison d'être* for the existence of the Gunung Kidul colony.

The work reserved for members of deportation colonies was naturally of the lowest and coarsest kind. Faber related that the main task of the colony of convicts in the unhealthy marshlands near Surabaja was to keep burning the huge fire-beacons which guided ships through the treacherous coastal waters into the harbor. Keeping these giant fires burning day and night must have been a strenuous task, for the heat was scorching and the huge stock of wood-fuel had to be replenished constantly. Moreover, members of the colony had to tow incoming ships along the banks and thus many of them became able pilots. The convict colonies were divided into eight classes according to the progress each had made in terms of good conduct. It might take one more than one generation to reach the uppermost class and so to return to society again.[37] Faber lists a number of places used as deportation colonies, among others, Tjirebon, Pekalongan, Semarang, Demak and Surabaja which later became ordinary coastal towns; the districts of Tjaruban, Prijangan and Gunung Kidul are also listed,to which Lodaja, mentioned above, might be added; all these latter places were situated in forest areas. Perhaps this indicates the work the deportees had to do; in the coastal colonies they kept the great beacons burning, towed incoming ships

---

36 Note the similarity with the Balinese custom of purification of mothers who have borne twins of different sex (regarded as incest) who have to live for a definite number of days at the cemetery.

37 Faber, *op. cit.*, p. 15. It is a pity that Faber does not always mention the sources from which he draws his conclusions.

and perhaps also loaded and unloaded cargoes, and in the wooded areas their main task must have been cutting and transporting the wood. It is certain that convicts were used for the heavy work of transporting goods in the service of the state. They were called *wong gladag* or *patjakan*. A special officer of sufficiently high rank, the *wedana gladag*, was assigned to organize and control their work. The assignment of a *wedana* indicates the importance of the department. The heaviness of the task depended on the demands of the state as well as on the number of members in the colony. Work must have been organized on the basis of rotating work squads. Again according to Faber, the work squad, guards and overseers were convicts of the highest class, called Pinggirs (*pinggir* means rim, border), and traditionally they were allotted the task of watching over the convicts of lower class. The name Pinggir must have been given them because of their status on the periphery (*pinggir*) of ordinary society into which they would in due time be admitted.[38]

The origin of the group named Pinggirs as well as of the other two groups, the Kalangs and the Gadjah or Gadjahmati, is offered by another source. The Kalang people, so the story goes, were descendants of animals of the wilds — a wild sow and a male dog both married to human beings who had chosen the forests as their home. Another story tells us that they were men of the woods who, because of their habit of raiding the villages, were "tamed" by Sultan Agung of Mataram. The king decreed that they had to live in walled villages and that they were not allowed to have intercourse with ordinary people. They were renowned saddlemakers and ropetwisters.[39] Wood construction was also their specialty.

Still another story makes the Pinggir and Gadjah conquered tribes from the region of Balambangan in eastern East Java, who were forcibly moved in considerable numbers to Central Java. From them were recruited men for a special corps of guardsmen, the Pradjurit Balambangan, because of their courage in battle. They were even ordered to serve, at one time, in testing the powers of newly forged krisses. It is certain that their womenfolk served as wetnurses for the royal infants. Their bluish milk was regarded as being exceedingly healthy. The name Pinggir might then

---

38 *Ibid.*, p. 24.
39 Inggris, "De Kalang's in Bagelen," *Djawa*, Vol. 1 (1921), no. 1, p. 32.

refer to *pinggir seganten* (the "rim of the sea," the coast), their original habitat.[40] We might conclude that these peoples were primitive tribes, perhaps of Pre-Dravidian or Proto-Malayan stock living in the deep forests or marshy coasts of Central and East Java originally. The Mataram rulers and undoubtedly also earlier kings exploited their special skills but it is apparent — since they were forced to live apart — that they were regarded as people of low caste, fit only to live with the undesirables of the common society. To be compelled to live and associate with these people really must have been a grave punishment for the status-conscious Javanese.

Nevertheless it could not be denied that these classes of people, convicts as well as the "aboriginal" groups, were an important economic factor in state life, which necessitated the assignment of officers with the high *wedana* or *najaka* rank,[41] although later the name "kabupaten Kalang" and "kabu-paten Gladag" referred more to the task and duties of the departments of respectively forest exploitation and transportation than to the specific group of people assigned to do the work.

Summarizing what we have tried to explain above about the acquisition and distribution of wealth in Later Mataram we may come to the conclusion that:

1. The taxation and labor-levy systems, like the organizational line of the state, were relatively simple and might be termed *ad hoc* or contingent financing.

2. The greatest source of state wealth had been trade and commerce, but after the total breakdown of trade because of Dutch competitive interference it had to become the peasantry,and so the wealth-gathering system became unbearably oppressive.

3. Labor exactions from the people formed a crucial economic factor for the functioning of the state.

40 S. Soehari, "Pinggir," *Djawa*, Vol. 9 (1929), nos. 3-4-5, pp. 161-168. Compare also Pigeaud's explanation in his *Java in the 14th Century*, Vol. IV, p. 419.

41 Rouffaer, *op. cit.*, pp. 54, 63.

ASTA BRATA

(The Eight Statesman's Virtues)

And please remember the eight duties;
be certain that they are within you
and like them, one by one.

Eight [virtues] must be within your body;
you must certainly not try to ignore them,
not even one of the eight.
Your kingship will be flawed
if one of the eight should be left out.
The first one is god Endra.
God Surja is the second.

Baju the third.
Kuwera forms the fourth one,
Baruna, the fifth;
Jama, Tjandra and Brama
complete the eight. Be sure that they are within the king,
his body, living, the Asta Brata,
true to a monarch.

As for the ways of *batara* Endra:
it is he who showers the earth with scent;
his benevolence spreading far and wide
evenly over the earth's face,
to the high and the low alike,

with no exceptions,
that truly is Endra's character.

That you must do, my brother,
to all of your subjects who populate the earth.
As for the one who acts against those who are evil
as their punisher,
who destroys all the malevolents in the realm
without distinguishing kin or clan;
if a man is evil, he shall then be killed.

Those who do evil
will be tracked and hunted down;
everywhere they will be followed relentlessly
and when caught, put to death.
All dirt of the state, he tries to sweep away.
Such is *batara* Jama,
in his efforts to safeguard the realm.

Thieves are the blemish of the state;
to get rid of the bad which soils [the kingdom],
all the king's officials must be ordered
not to house the bad
and he who favors acts of evil must leave.
The bad will be killed
until all their kind are annihilated entirely —

all kinds of evil acts.
And in this, you really must practice god Jama's [ways].
Surja is the third;
the way of *paramarta* is his,
showering grace and kindness [while he]
lets his intention penetrate [the heart],
peacefulness being the sole aim.

Be without fierceness, do not follow passion.
Your officials will not feel your command if you aim

for the good.
There will not be any difficulty [if you]
go under [cover] to reach your aim.
What you want to have, try to gain it with tact and in so doing you will
have what you want.

Do not be hasty in trying to attain your wish.
Even if a man is not sharp of mind his heart can always
      be reached;
[Your command] will not lose its aim because it is imposed
      with care.
Fourth is the way of god Tjandra;
forgivingness forms his instrument
filling the whole earth.

Aiming at the contentedness of the whole kingdom,
in his reign he is full of kindness in his heart;
all of his words express such an attitude
so do his countenance and his behavior.
His acts are always accompanied with a smile,
never showing any strain,
showing his charm in all his commands.

[A feeling of] intrinsic peace towards humanity
reigns in his heart, through and through;
kindhearted, intensely beloved
by all ascetics.
The fifth one is the way of *batara* Baju:
determined to understand what is done in the world,
the universe's will he tries to grasp.

Without limit or boundary
are his efforts to know the intention of
all his officers — unnoticed he does it —
evil as well as their good intentions
all of his dignitaries' actions he can see.

While earning their living,
his officers constantly live in prosperity.
Never ceasing is [the king's] striving
for the happiness of his men
and for the good of them
their hearts he beseeches
in order to achieve prosperity and peace.

In their hearts they cannot make a move
which [the king] will not see clearly;
excellence and noble conduct are followed,
good morals and happiness.
His superior character is unanimously accepted.
That is Baju's way of life.
Please, keep it in mind constantly.

The sixth is god Kuwera,
always giving prosperity and happiness.
In applying his means
he never uses physical contact
towards those to whom he entrusts the navigation of the
        [ship] of state;
he benefits them [fully] in
their efforts to do no wrong.

The whole realm he entrusts [to them].
Free flowing are his gifts, superhuman
ability forms his constant aim
he never praises nor blames;
to all he does the same.
In his trust the whole knowledge of knighthood he gives
        [to his men],
while they do not know that their innermost self is being studied [by the king].

The seventh is Baruna.
Always with a weapon he goes through life

in order to find security on the road.
In his heart he always concentrates
to master all the power of magic
even to the extent of wiping out all world's content.
Excelling in insight and full of caution,

wiping away all the crooked.
Sad and afraid are the men of bad living.
The whole earth is under his rule;
known to him is what is bad and what is good.
Never hesitant in applying the remedy,
unyielding in his virtue;
you certainly must take Baruna as an example.

The way of life of god Brama:
the worldly needs he seeks to acquire, with all his men,
        whether high or low of rank.
Brutal he is against the enemy.
He knows the habits of his troops.
Blown away will the enemy be, overwhelmed and ground down.
Follow the example of god Brama;
be his — be in accordance with your heart.

(From Kyai Jasadipoera *Serat Rama*, Semarang,
1919, p. 432ff.

abdi — servant

abdidalem — persons in the service of the king

adil paramarta — just but not harsh

adipati — high title, rank

adja sok njepelekake — do not belittle

adjeg — 1. regular; 2. fixed

adoh — far

agama — religion

agami — (Kr) see *agama*

ageming ratu — to be worn by a king

ageng — (Kr) big

agung — lofty, high positioned

ahli — expert

ajang-ajang — shadow

alit — (Kr) small

alun-alun — open square before the residence of a high dignitary

andana warih — of noble birth

andaru — blue fireball foreboding rank or position

angger — law

angker — imbued with evil influences (of places)

asaur peksi djumurung — unanimously approved

asrama — hermitage

asta — eight

awatara — incarnation (of gods)

babad — 1. to clear (woods); 2. history

badut — clown

bahu — 1. unit of arable land; 2. worker, helper

bakal — basic material (clothing, wood)

baku — basic

bala — 1. in the king's service; 2. the army

banda-bandu — "wealth and kin " expressing ultimate wealth

bandar — toll stop

bang kulon — western realm

bang wetan — eastern realm

banteng — wild bull

banter — 1. fast (speed); 2. consistent (of *tapa*)

batara — title of a god

bati — profit

batur tukon — bought slave

bau — see *bahu*

bawon — pay in kind at harvesting

beja — duty (at the customs)

bekel — 1. someone holding a lease on land of an appanage holder; 2. lower official

bekel gundul — a *bekel* without men to extract labor from

bendara — the king's close relatives; see *sentana*

bengkok — "salary-field" of an official; see *lungguh*

binatara — honored like a *batara*

brata — way of life

bubuka saking agama — because of religion

buda — old, from the Hinduistic period

budi — 1. intellect; 2. disposition

budjang — bachelor

bujut — .1. title of veneration for old people; 2. great grandparents

bupati — high dignitary

çakti — (Skrt)

chakravarttin -(Skrt) see *tjakrawati*

dadi — to become

dalang — *wajang* puppeteer

dampar kentjana — golden stool

dana — alms, gifts

dawa kuntjarane — far does its fame reach

demang — lower official

desa — Javanese village

dewa — deity

dina sangar — day of ill luck (astrology)

dipati — see *adipati*

djabarangkah — the outer regions

djadjahan — dependency, colony

djaga — watch-duty

djagade — its realm, its sphere

djakat — religious gift

djaksa — attorney

djaman kala bendu — age of misfortune

Djawi — (Kr) Java, Javanese

djedjer — 1. principle; 2. scene

djeksa — see *djaksa*

djubah — overcoat

djumbuhing kawula gusti — principle of one-ness between man and God

djumurung — to agree

djung — 28,386 square metres

dupak budjang, semu mantri, esem bupati — a kick for a servant, an insinuation for a *mantri*, a smile for a regent (the higher the position, the more subtle the reprimand)

dusun — *desa*, village

duwur — high

ejang — grandparent

embanan — setting (of a ring)

empu — title of one with great professional skill

esem — a smile

firasat — physiognomy

gadung — climbing plant with edible but stupefying tubers

gamelan — Javanese orchestra

gara-gara — disturbance of nature

garebeg — the three important Moslem holy festivals of Mulud, Pasa and Besar

gawe — 1. work; 2. feast

gawe-desa — *desa*-duties

gede obore, padang djagade, duwur kukuse — expression denoting outstanding fame

gedong — building

gilig — 1. to come to complete agreement; 2. rounded

glebagan — turnover of shares of communal land

gogol — villager shareholder of communal land

gotong-rojong — system of mutual help

gugur-gunung — coming out of the whole population in case of calamities

gundul — bald

gung — great, from *agung*, see *ageng*

gunung kendeng, semune kenya musoni — saying indicating old age and fussiness

guru — teacher, particularly of spiritual matters

gusti — master, lord

hadith — Moslem tradition as source of theological interpretation

hyang — title of a deity

iladuni — secret knowledge, especially prophesying

isi lan wadah — content and receptacle

isjwara — instruction, indication

isnad — proof of authenticity (Moslem tradition)

kadigdajan — immunity to weapons or magic spell

kaendran — Indra's heaven

kagempalaken — broken off from

kakawin surti — kind of instructive poetry

kalabendu — period of disaster and malady

kali yuga — world-period of decline

kalipatullah — caliphate

kalpa sru semune kenaka putung — indication of a reign of anger and cruelty

kamantepan — consistency

kamukten — state of being endowed with richness and prestige

kanda — spoken recital in *wajang* play

kang tjedak manglung, kang adoh tumijung — indicating voluntary submission to benevolent rule of a king

kanigara — fez-like black velvet headgear with linear gold-leaf ornamentation

kantor — office

kapit — between something

kapradjuritan — pertaining to

literature

karemenan — consistency and loyalty

karja — 1. work; 2. unit of arable land

karman — (Skrt) work, deed

karsaning Pangeran — God's will

kasampurnan — ultimate perfection

katekan — attained (of aim)

kauripan — with the property of restoring life

kawibawan — authority

kawirjan — nobility

kawula-gusti — Man-God (relationship)

kawulawisuda — installed to a high position

kenaka — fingernail

kenja — girl

kentjana — gold

keparak — certain group of officials at court

kerata-basa — word interpretation according to sound in folk etymology

kerigan — general call to arms or at great disasters

kerisan — wearing a kris

ketoprak — Javanese operetta with unlimited repertory of indigenous or foreign stories

kewales — to suffer the consequences of one's deed

ki bujut — title of veneration

ki sanak — used towards strangers

kiwa — left

kotang Antakusuma — name of a relic in the form of a jacket

Krama Inggil — highest honorific form of Javanese speech

krotjokan — a "come one come all"

kraton — palace

ksatria — knight

kukuh — strongly built

kulawisuda — see *kawulawisuda*

kuli kendo — second category of villagers, see *tumpang*

kuli kentjeng, kuli sikep — first category of villagers

kulon — west

kuluk — fez-like headgear

kusuma — flower

kyai — title of veneration, also *kyageng*

labuh — ceremony of offering to sea or stream spirits

laku — see *lampah*

lambang pradja — state symbol

lampah — (Kr) a life of

lampah sandi — secretly

lan — and

lanang — male

lapa — hunger

lara-lapa — misery and hunger

leluhur — ancestors

lenga kauripan — oil of life

lokapala — the eight Guardians of the universe

lor — north

ludruk — king of folk-operetta in East Java

luhur — 1. of high birth; 2. of great wisdom

lung — tendril

lungguh — appanage, salary-field, see *bengkok*

lurah — 1. master, lord; 2. village headman

lurah sentana — prince, head of the king's kin

lurah tledek — chief of the public dancing girls

madeg kraman — to revolt

madjupat — four-cornered

madu — honey

madya — middle

magang — apprentice

mandala — territorial circle of political influence

mandjing — to go into and be one with something

manglung — to bow down to

mantjalima — the *mantjapat* with the villages next to them

mantjanegara — outlying regions of the kingdom

mantjapat — the four neighboring villages, houses

mantri — official of lower rank

manunggal — to become one (with God)

mata pitaja — confidant, spy

matjan-gadungan — were-tiger

mawas obah osiking bala — to keep an eye on the wishes of his people

mbalela — to revolt

mbalik — to revolt, to turn

mbaudenda mjakrawati — mighty and influential (of a king)

mbebeneri — to do justice

mbeka — to revolt, to be recalcitrant

midji — special (of a task)

momong — to take care of (a child, one's wife)

momongan — the person taken care of; see *pamong*

mondong — to carry

muksa — to disappear with one's physical body

murba-wisesa — to have the power of decision

murwa — to begin

musoni — to clean (rice, cotton)

naga — mythical serpent

nagara — state

nagaragung — the inner realms, the core region

najaka — high-ranking officer

narawita — lands excluded for special purposes

ndedagan — keeping watch at a grave to acquire spiritual power

ndjaga tata-tentreming pradja — guarding the peace and tranquillity of the state

negara — see *nagara*

neges karsaning hyang ingkang murbeng pandulu — trying to comprehend God's will by fasting, ascetic practice

ngadili — to do justice

nganglang — going the rounds to control the realm

ngelar djadjahan — to expand the realm through conquest

ngelmu — knowledge, especially secret knowledge

ngenger — to serve with a family of high position

ngestreni — to attend (a wedding)

nglikasi — to reel (weaving)

ngoko — Low Javanese

ngreka — to arrange

nila — indigo

niti — 1. to inspect; 2. tact

nitis — to reincarnate

njakrawati — see *tjakrawati*

njamur kawula — incognito

njuwita — to serve (in a family)

nungkul — to bow, to surrender nur — light, divine light nurbuwah — divine sign of prophecy

obah — to move

obore — its torch

osik — unexpressed thought

padang — light

padjeg — tax

padjeg-bumi — land tax

pakadja — 1. the lotus flower; 2. a semi-precious stone

paken — outlines of *wajang* stories

palak palakijah — astrology

palawidja — 1. products planted after rice; 2. deformed persons in the king's retinue

pamong — the person taking care (of a child, one's wife); see *momongan*

pamong pradja — the civil service

pamoring gusti-kawula — the merging of man into God

pamrih — with benefit as motive

pamudjan — place of worship

panakawan — valet, companion

panantang — the challenge

pandita — sage

pandulu — look, glance

panembahan — title of persons of high rank or spiritual knowledge

panengen — see *tengen*

pangajoman — protection

pangeran dipati — prince, crown-prince

pangiwa — see *kiwa*

pangreh pradja — the civil service, all the king's officials of the "outer" (territorial) service

pangulon — Office of Religious Affairs under a *pangulu*

pangulu naib — clerical rank under the *pangulu*

pangurakan — place around the main gate to the *alun-alun*

panjuwun — petition, request

pantjen — personal service to digni-taries (of villagers)

papa — needy, in misery.

paprentahan — government

para bendara — the king's kin

para luhur — the nobility

paringan — gift

paron — half and half

pasar — market

pasarejan — cemetery

pasir — sand

pasir-wukir — coast and highlands

pasisir — coastal regions

pati — 1. lord; 2. death

patih — grand vizier

patih ndjaba — *patih* of the "outer" service (the realm)

patih ndjero — *patih* of the "inner" service (the court)

patjakan — see *wong gladak*

peksi — 1. bird"; 2. part of the kris, the hilt

penggede — high official

pengulu — see *pangulon*

perang desa — "village war," disorders as a result of Mataram's division in 1755

perdikan — free-village

pesantren — institution for Moslem religious instruction

petang palak palakijah — astrological calculations (knowledge)

piagem — charter, decree

pikulan — carrying-pole, load

pinesti — pre-ordained

pinggir — rim, border

pitaja — trust

pitrah — religious alms for the poor

piwulang — lesson, ethical instruction

pondok — boarding house (of a *pesantren*)

prabu — title of king

pradja — the state

pradjurit — warrior, soldier

pralaja — the Great Upheaval, Götterdämmerung

pralambang — (God's) sign or indication of things to come

praptane kalabendu ing Semar-ang lan Tembajat — the coming of mishap will be at Semarang and Tembajat (a *pralambang*)

prijaji — the king's officials, forming the Javanese elite

pundutan — see *taker turun*

punggawa — officials not of noble blood

pulung — lightball as a divine sign of a high position or rank to come

pusaka — holy inherited objects

putra — offspring

putung — broken in two

raden — title of the king's relatives from the fifth grade down

radja — king

rame — bustling

randu alas — giant wild "kapok"-cotton tree (bombax malabaricum)

rangkah — 1. barricade; 2. tollgate at the boundaries of the state

rara — maiden

ratu — king

ratu adil — the coming Messiah

ratu gung binatara — Great Ruler

ratu sewu negara — the thousand kings bowing to the rule of a great emperor

redi — (Kr) mountain

reh pangulon — under the jurisdiction of the *pangulu's* office

rembesing madu — of noble birth

resi — hermit

sabil — war to propagate Islam

sabrang — a foreign country, another island (than Java)

sada lanang — nerve of the leaf of a certain palm

saderek — (Kr) relative

sahbandar — harbormaster

saking — (Kr) from

salere — north of

sanak — relative

sandi — secret code

sang murba-wisesa — "the one who has the right to decide and punish" (title of the king)

sanga — nine

sangar — having evil influence (a place, certain hours of certain days)

sanggar pamudjan — place of meditation

sapa — who

sasrahan — see *bawon*

satak — certain amount of money

sawetaning gunung Lawu — east of Mount Lawu

seba — to come to audience

sedija — prepared to

sedjarah panengen — the "right"

line of lineage of the Mataram kings

sedjarah pangiwa — the "left" line of lineage of the Mataram kings

sekti — with superhuman powers

semedi — to meditate

semune — the allusion is…

senapati — commander in chief

senenan — tournaments on horseback on Monday (*Senen*)

sentana — the king's more distant relatives; see *bendara*

sepele — insignificant, very easy

sepi ing pamrih, rame ing gawe — free of the desire for gain, full of activity

serat — (Kr) letter

serban — turban

seru — loud

sesotya — jewel, precious stone

sesupe — (Kr) ring

seton — tournament on horseback, held on Saturday (*Setu*) as part of military training; see *senenan*

setunggil — one

sewu — thousand

sideku — sitting with elbows resting on the knees

sila — sitting cross-legged before a superior

sinengkakake ing ngaluhur — raised to a high position

sing sapa gede panjuwune, bakal katekan sedyane — he who sincerely asks (of God) will reach his goal singa — lion

sirna — disappear without a trace

siti dusun salere redi Kendeng — regions north of the Kendeng range

sruwal — underpants

suksma — soul

suluk — 1. chanted interludes by the puppeteer at a *wajang* play to set the mood of the act; 2. secret teachings in Islamic mysticism

sultan — sultan

sunan — title of a king or that of a Wali

surasa — deeper or inner meaning

suruh — leaf as ingredient in betel-nut chewing

suwun — 1. to ask; 2. to carry on one's head

svadharma — (Skrt) destination

taker turun — side-taxes

tanah sabrang — the other islands

tandon — what is carried in a sedan-chair

tapa — ascetic practice

tatatjara — custom, tradition

tebih — far

tedaking andana warih — of august descent

tegalan — dry, unirrigated lands

teges — meaning

tekad — determination

tekdir — fate

teluh bradja — fire-ball as an omen of disease to come

tengen — right

tentrem — tranquil, calm

tepa-slira — to estimate to one's own capacity

tijang alit — the common people

tinitah — ordained, destined

tiwikrama — demonic rage

tjadong — ration

tjahja nurbuwah — *nurbuwah* light, see *nurbuwah*

tjakra — Kresna's disc-shaped weapon

tjakrawati — world rule

tjandi — temple from the Hindu period

tjantang-balung — palace-dancers, doing clownish dances at processions

tjara — way (of life)

tjarangan — "branch"-story of the *wajang*

tjatjah — 1.notch; 2. number of able, male shareholders of communal land in a certain region; 3. measurement of land for taxation

tjaton — see *tjatu*

tjatu — one share

tjedak — close

tjengkal — approx. 3.75 m.

tjuriga — the kris

tobat — to repent

topeng — mask

trahing kusuma — of noble birth

trasi — fish-paste

triman — women given as a wife to an official by the king as a favor tumbal — magically potent objects to ward off evil

tumenggung — high title, lower than *adipati*

tumijung — to bow, to" hang over

tumpang — third category of villagers

tumpang slosor, pondok slosor — fourth category of villagers, see *kuli*

tuna — loss

tuwan — sir, mister

ukum — law, religious law

unggul — winning

upatjara — 1. regalia of Javanese kings; 2. ceremony

uwal — to become detached from

Vorstenlanden — (D) Dutch name given to the two Javanese kingdoms of Surakarta and Jogjakarta

wadah — receptacle

wadi — secret

wahju — divine token of greatness and honor

wajang — Javanese shadow-play

wajang-wujungan — going to and fro in great disorder

wali — a saint

warana — screen

warangka — scabbard of a kris

warih — water

waringin — giant banyan tree (ficus benghalensis)

warta — news, message

waskita — clairvoyant

wedana — 1. chief-*bupati*;

2. district officer under a *bupati* wenang — authorized, having the right

wetan — east

wewaler — taboo

widjining tapa — descendant of an ascetic

wisesa — might, power

wisuda — to inaugurate

witjaksana — tactful, wise

wong — man

wong gladag — men of the transport department

wong tjilik — the common people

wukir — mountain

(D) = Dutch

(Kr) = Krama; High Javanese

(Skrt) = Sanskrit

MAP ONE
MATARAM - DECREASE OF TERRITORY

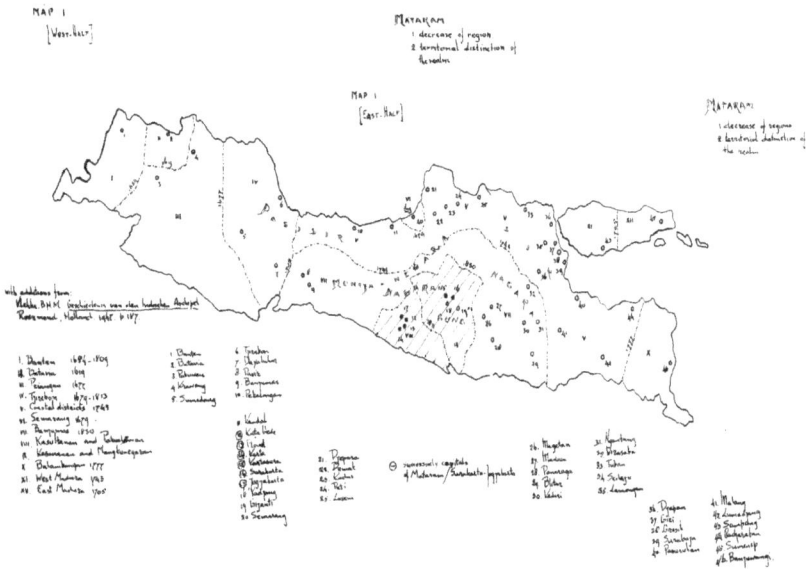

M A P   T W O
MATARAM - NAMES OF REGIONS

www.ingramcontent.com/pod-product-compliance
Lightning Source LLC
Chambersburg PA
CBHW020001290326
41935CB00007B/260